International Management

Getting your head out of the managerial cloud

Kevin Griffiths

ISBN:1475113978
ISBN-13:978-1475113976

DEDICATION

For Franciska, Rebecca, Lucas, Victoria, Cassandra, Olivia,
Noah and Isabella

CONTENTS

ACKNOWLEDGMENTS

Without any doubt I would have never completed this paper without the support and encouragement of my wife Franciska. A big thank you to you and our children Rebecca, Lucas, Victoria, Cassandra, Olivia, Noah and Isabella for giving me the time, space , understanding and love needed to complete this task. Your sacrifice does not go unappreciated.

Thanks also to The University of Liverpool and Laureate Education who provided the motivation and resources for me to complete this work during my studies for a MSc in International Management.

Introduction - Art or Science?

Management is seen as a fundamental part of human social environment and modern organisation. To define management as an art or science it is necessary to recognise the basic instinct and structure of human organisation. Chi-Kuo Mao (n.d) "A human organization exists as a process of creative advancement in which the organization ceaselessly defines itself and sustains itself." The managers access to various managerial theories requires an element of instinctive response to accommodate the motivational needs of the individual. By employing instinctive human understanding to guide the manager towards a more effective way of achieving organisational goals, we could say that the act of reading or understanding of the person or situation is an art. Art meaning creative interaction with fellow human beings and the science as the structural process of implementation towards the organisational goal.

To reason that management is both art and science we should look at the role played by both in achieving the goals of the organisation. If the science part of management is the structured, planed and defined part of the organisations strategy we should remember that theories change. In the paper "Managing Complex Organizations: Complexity Thinking and Science and Art Management" Richardson (2008) quotes Maxwell "Any scientific theory, however well it has been verified empirically, will always have infinitely many rival theories that fit the available evidence just as well but that make different predictions, in an arbitrary way, for yet unobserved phenomena. (Maxwell, 2000) Therefore it becomes necessary to adapt to the changing environment and theoretical approaches.

To apply the element of art to the process it would be reasonable to say that it is the act of relaying the vision of the strategy, by the manager, that motivates people. The CEO, the Entrepreneur, for example holds an artistic responsibility to interpret and communicate his or her vision in a manner that can be related to by all organisational members?

It could be reasonable to assume that the art element discussed here is in fact the art of leadership. If this is the case then it would be natural to assume that good management involves strong leadership and creative communication of scientific concepts.

Using art as an explanation for the inspirational element and science as the delivery mechanism makes sense in terms of the understanding of the managerial processes. Encapsulating both instinctive human interaction and by employing strategies that are based on known theories, and there effectiveness, we can apply a reasonable assumption that making people more effective through imparting vision is art and the way in which they achieve that vision is by a route of structured theory, the science.

Chapter 1

Introduction to Strategic Organization

The nature and purpose of business organisation

All companies should strive to achieve a status of competitive advantage. The ability to maintain that status in a world that is becoming more decentralized and de-regularized is dependent on the superior organisation of the company. That is, an organisation that can adapt and evolve to meet the needs of is customer base while maintaining motivation amongst its staff. While products and services can be developed to fit market trends, Child (2005) points out "Organization, on the other hand, is an asset that each company has to develop to suit its needs and situation, and it cannot be bought of the self." It is the structuring and implementation of an organisation that will determine its success within its marketplace. When the marketplace changes it is necessary for the organisation to modify or completely change its approach to that market. We can see that Danish hearing aid producer Oticon (Broody, 2008) faced massive competition in the eighties. To maintain and improve its competitive advantage it changed from an industrial organisation to a service organisation, from a base of specialists to a work force that could develop many skills. It moved from a hierarchical to horizontal organisational structure. This was a necessary move to facilitate the success of the company. One could argue that this was not a superior organisation but it evolved into one, however, Child (2008) identifies other factors that influence organisations, these are history, nationality, leadership and reputation. It is these factors that allowed the company to change it organisational structure and maintain its position in the marketplace.

Rather than a superior organisation being one that adapts to the market one could argue that it is a company that drives and manipulates the marketplace for its competitive advantage that is the superior. In a case study Broody (2008) it is seen that when Nokia entered the mobile phone market in the 1990's, apart from the standardization of the GSM system in Europe, Nokia had identified that mobile phones were more than phones, they were fashion accessories and design was the factor that gave them the competitive advantage resulting in a market share of around 35%. They were the drivers of the market.

While it is easy to see that the organisation of a company and its ability to change rapidly in todays international environment is the key to gaining and maintaining competitive advantage it would be interesting to see how a company could loose its position. As CEO of a small start-up low cost airline due to start operating out of Granada, Spain I have experienced a drastic fall from competitive advantage to competitive dis-advantage. With approximately 3 months to the launch, we were the only airline to fly to the UK and Northern Europe from Granada. One morning I came into work and discovered that Irish low-cost carrier Ryanair would be flying into Granada. Their position of strength in terms of organisation and financial power meant that we were not in a position to compete. Ryanair's time in the low cost airline sector as given it a distinct advantage over its competitors. Its organisational structure and business model is a powerful tool in driving the trends of air travel in Europe, another example of companies driving the market.

I can say that superior organisations can only sustain a competitive advantage when when they are adaptive to market changes, those that set the market may be in a superior position now but the test will come when external forces dictate a change, it is then we will see if they are truly have a superior organisational structure that can maintain competitive advantage.

Strategic organisation to meet new challenges

Knowledge Workers are the new fertilizers of modern organisational structure and market development. Because companies and organisations operate in a global environment, embedded with technology, that facilitates a rapid exchange of information, there is a need to rapidly and creatively respond to market trends and needs. Using the more traditional hierarchical structures is prohibitive to the delivery of effective timely solutions because of the slow transit of information through the bureaucratic environment. To achieve a more responsive organisation Ehin (2008) states, "Fundamentally, we need to discover that in the Knowledge Age, it is much more advantageous to give up hierarchical control in order to gain much greater self-regulating order and participation throughout an organization."

One of the first companies to inspire me with a flatter organisational structure, and one that adopted a policy of knowledge and innovation development was 3M. Brand (1998) outlines the basis of the companies philosophy "3M sees Knowledge Management more as a cultural and organizational issue than a technological one." It is the manner in which knowledge workers are supported, encouraged and managed that leads to effective delivery within the market. One of the more successful elements for promoting innovation is the 15% rule. This is where workers are encouraged to spend 15% of their work time on their own innovative ideas that fall outside of the their normal work areas. Brand (1998) confirms the successful nature of this policy "The consequence of this 15% rule has been a number of important new businesses for the company."

While one can see the impact and success of the flatter organisational structures that encourage creativity there should be some concern that it could develop into a solely ideas based and not delivery based system. When organisations encourage too much democratic debate or failure to self-regulate there is a possibility of indecision. At some point there needs to be a mechanism for a decision to be made. In fact Ehin (2008) places organizational structures into just two general categories: controlled- and shared-access systems. With shared-access system, "situational leadership emerges based on expert knowledge" while with controlled access "one individual or a very limited number of people exclusively control access to all major resources." When leadership mechanisms are in place, the fulfillment of an organisations knowledge workers can be delivered, providing that the connection between the knowledge worker and the organisations goals are the same.

We can see that even if you engage the idea of Ehins two organisational structures it is important for companies to foster ideas and innovation within an environment of open access and knowledge transfer. This is a fundamental factor in responding to and implementing change in a diverse global market. Child (2005) says that "In order to cope with high velocity and make strategic decisions with corresponding speed, firms need to be organized so as to provide decision makers with more information and the capacity to develop more alternatives, as well as to promote integration and conflict resolution among decision makers" 3M's 15% rule identifies the individuals freedom to develop ideas but also accommodates the structure to ensure good delivery of marketable concepts.

Globalization as potentially had more impact on industry and business in terms of social impact than the industrial revolution. Wright (1998) concludes "that globalization is a real and significant force for change affecting organisations strategy, operations and characteristics " This technological and communication revolution as resulted in the need for companies and organisations to adopt systems of management that can develop and respond quickly to markets. Being unable to respond efficiently to competition and changes in the well informed and fickle customer base will result in loss of market share and eventually failure. Former hierarchical structures based on historical practices are unable to respond quickly to changes in approaches by competitors that result in market share loss. Although the need to adapt to compete is not new as Roberts (2004) identifies with the account of how the Hudson Bay Company was challenged by the North West Company. North West had identified and established better systems for serving its customers and reacting "on the ground" to changing factors. Hudson was stuck in a bureaucratic environment with slow communications and slow reaction times, which resulted in losing the competitive advantage.

In the modern world of hyper-competition the need for firms to be fluid and responsive in and to its operating environment is paramount. This as resulted in many organisations radically restructuring, not only in terms of staffing and departmental structure, but also in corporate culture and ethos. The company needs to ensure it is able to respond rapidly and appropriately to its target audience. This target audience is both internal, the employees,, and external, the customer. This has been one of the driving factors that has guided Southwest Airlines to be a ground breaker in the aviation industry. To accommodate the need for fast reaction times firms need to foster creativity through openness, communication structure, sustainable relationships and diversified decision making. Gittell, (2002) shows that "Southwest's most distinctive organizational competency is its ability to build and sustain relationships characterized by shared goals, shared knowledge, and mutual respect." Southwest's business model has been the bedrock of the development of Low Cost Carriers around the world, however, the transference of their model has not necessarily been successful in all cases, primarily within the " old school" flag carrier airlines. This is probably due to the fact that they followed the "no frills fast turn around policy" without looking deeper into the corporate culture of Southwest. Child (2005) highlights that other airlines "have been unable to replicate Southwest's success largely because they have not adopted its approach to organization and people"

By looking deeper into the organisational structure, ethos and the methods of motivating and valuing employees Southwest have succeeded in creating a sustainable structure that meets the needs of the modern traveller, and, by being open, fluid and supportive with its staff, it is in a stronger position to meet future challenges in the industry. This has manifested in Southwest being in a strong financial position even during significant negative influences within the travel sector, namely 9/11 and the increase in fuel costs. This points out that for companies to be successful they need to understand that it is not only the end product that creates market position but that the support and shared vision of the employees are also key drivers to success.

On occasions it may require a more radical approach to adapt an organisation to survive in difficult market and economic conditions. This was the case with Brazilian company Semco. On taking over the company in 1982 Ricardo Semlar undertook a radical reshaping and dismantling of the companies management and organisational structure. The new focus was to create a flexible employee focused environment with profit sharing, employee participation and free flowing open information.(Broddy, 2008) The new system relies on the loyalty and commitment of the employees for the company to function fully. In fact by devolving power and decision making responsibility to the workforce, Semco reduced from12 layers of management to 3, the entire operation managed to allow the company to ride out the Brazilian economic crisis of the 1990's. Staff cross trained and performed several roles within the company all of which was self managed. This new approach of empowering the workforce was highlighted by Crainer (1999) Semco takes workplace democracy to previously unimagined frontiers. "Everyone at the company has access to the books; managers set their own salaries; shop floor workers set their own productivity targets and schedules; workers make decisions that were once the preserve of managers; even the distribution of the profit sharing scheme is determined by employees".The fulfillment of the corporate vision is the responsibility of all employees. Encouraging employee loyalty will help equip a company to deal with lean times. People who feel they are a valid part of the organisation will go the "extra mile" to ensure the survival of the firm. Pay cuts, extra unpaid work, varied task.

Both Southwest and Semco have taken the bold steps to meet the needs of modern trading scenarios. It is by taking these steps and imparting faith in the workforce that the success of these companies can serve to inspire others. While the Semco story is inspiring and has been explored by many it may be a little too radical for some, however, it is not a unique in structure. There are many organisations that operate from a fully democratic and collective responsibility, in particular the cooperative movement. The strength of the company is not completely dominated by structure and organisation but by the people who are valued and heard within that structure. This is demonstrated by the financial success and staff retention of both companies. For continuing success of these companies it could be said there is a need to 'stay allergic to hierarchy". Cook (2004) quotes Dell (1999).

Integration as a strategic response

Transference of information across an organisations supply chain is critical for effective customer service. Using an integrated communication system combined with a free flowing, two way responsive culture, will go a long way to ensure a customer focused reactive delivery process. With the hierarchical organisations becoming the dinosaurs of modern business the newer flatter structures need to ensure all areas of operation are in "the Loop". Achieving a high level of integration becomes a paramount part of the organisational strategy in maintaining appropriate levels of awareness within the organisations supply chain. Along with high levels of accessibility to information it is also beneficial to have a multi-disciplinary workforce with departmental crossover. Strategic partners must also fall into the knowledge communication exchange to ensure continuity of product development and delivery.

Significant levels of change need to take place within the culture of an organisation during the change of operating structures. Employees and management must adopt a thinking process outside of their direct area of operation. If we look at the process of integration through business process management we see that the elements of Design, Modeling, Execution, Monitoring and then optimization will deliver critical processes within the supply chain ensuring that customer/ client needs are met through fast accurate response times. Goldkuhl and Lind (2008) recall that Keen and Knapp (1996) have noted that there are two contrasted different views on business processes; "process as workflow" vs "process as the coordination of work". These differing definitions do not in my opinion contradict each other. Both are crucial for total awareness and efficient output across the supply chain. Team elements that ensure fast flow delivery and coordination between different operational elements of the organisation will help give the competitive advantage.

As Child (2005) points out there are within a more formal approach three mechanisms to integration i) standardization. The establishment of rules. ii) bureaucratic mechanisms. To develop and implement plans and strategy. iii) Formal Standing. The formation of a committee. He goes on to say" By formulating a body of procedures and operating plans, the contributions of separate departments can be clearly specified and so integrated into the task of the organisation as a whole". The concept of a free thinking solution orientated work force operating in an environment of rules and regulations may seem a little alien, but, procedural protocols do ensure continuity within the supply chain and therefore are necessary.

Many years ago I worked for a branch of the British Red Cross. At the time I joined the organisation was in fact approximately 50 individual, separately registered charities. Each branch took advice but not direction from "Head Quarters" This created a tremendous disadvantage in not only delivering services efficiently across the the country but also from a PR marketing and ultimately a fund-raising point of view. It was decided that all of the branches would be merged into one organisation. This raised issues around implementing change but also tackling the issue of clear consistent flow of information. Integration through the establishment of regional teams that feed into the volunteer supporters gave a much more consistent resource. Volunteers are a good example of multi disciplinary work force at the delivery point of the organisation. By capitalizing on the skill base of the volunteers within a more lateral structure the organisation has succeeded in delivering better national services to those in need.

The assumption that organisational structures change to suit the changing environment, thus allowing more responsive reactions to market conditions, is valid when existing organisational structures are unable to accommodate such changes due to inefficient internal mechanisms. These changes to structure are not solid forms that will meet the needs of the company permanently. New structures should be organic and fluid enough to facilitate reactions to internal and external fluctuations. Companies that operate in fast moving environments like telecoms faced significant threats with the deregulation in Europe. Traditional suppliers found themselves in a much more competitive environment. Significant changes were needed to accommodate customer demands and respond to emerging competition from small more flexible companies. McAdam and McCormack (2001) identify that "New suppliers, and new customers create new technologies, shorter product life-cycles and demand for quicker payback on investments" This was an environment that the more tradition telecom equipment suppliers found challenging. Indeed the need to face the issue was critical for survival. With telecom service providers embarking on international expansion the need for standardization of equipment across borders was a key factor in driving efficiency.

If we look at Nortel as an example of responsive approaches to meet the needs of its existing and new customers we see them embark on a strategy of accelerated merging of data and voice communications. McAdam and McCormack (2001) It recognized that there would be a merger of voice and data transmission and that the deregulation of the market would offer the potential for cross border strategic development with key players in the service delivery area, British Telecom and Telefonica. The resulting outcome was that Nortel Networks needed to become a customer focused organisation.

A process of rationalization of the companies manufacturing bases into a smaller interconnected supply and logistics operations was the result. Nortel's reduction in suppliers and more strategic relationships with those remaining to deliver globally played a significant role in achieving a strategic advantage. Nortel focused its operational structure to "seven system houses" one of these in Monkstown, Northern Ireland. Responsible for R&D, product development and marketing, logistics and customer relationships.

If a company needs to change its organisational structure to facilitate decisions based on fluctuations within its trading environment then it must ensure that those changes are sustainable within its supply chain strategy. When empowering staff to make strategical decisions it is imperative that they experience issues from several supply chain perspectives. As we can see from Nortel adoption of Manufacturing 2000 they continue to develop process based teams and as McAdam and McCormack (2001) state "The supply chain must be managed as a single organisation"

Strategic control and motivation

Nortels structural changes enabled it to develop its position within the global telecom market and at its peak employed over 2000 people at Monkstown. However, as a sign of how rapidly situations change Nortel faces a greater challenge today. Having filed for bankruptcy protection in the US and late last year announcing 1,300 job cuts worldwide and a $3.4 bn quarterly loss the company will need to "rethink" it structure again. A Nortel statement quoted in the Belfast Telegraph (2009) says "Nortel intends to emerge from this process as a more focused, financially sound and competitive company. This is a step towards a global reorganization of Nortel."

In conclusion we can say that changing your organisational structure to suit your environment is not a one stop operation. Solutions to market changes and difficulties are an evolution and it is only the fittest who will survive.

Strategically it is imperative that the methods of control within an organisation are harmonious with the culture and ethos of the company. Control can be identified as a means of ensuring that objectives are achieved. The models of control deployed by a company should be instrumental in achieving goals and motivating staff. Moving towards a delayered linear organisational structure means empowering members of that organisation. Attitudes to control will depend on each individual and their motivational activators. This requires that there is an awareness, from managers, of factors that drive key workers is a critical part of developing control systems.

Child (2005) proposes two levels of control within an organisation, strategic control and operational control. Strategic control involves the mechanisms, resources and future direction of the company. The way in that this area of control is executed can dictate the the form and success of the company. Simultaneously running is the area of operational control, a more rudimentary activity that functions on the more ambiguous area of motivational stimulation.

In Child's (2005) identification of six controlling strategical elements "cultural control" is an elemental part of implementing and succeeding in achieving operational goals in a modern educated freethinking workforce. It enables the other areas of control to be positively implemented within appropriate organisational structures. In fact within the fast moving strategically fluid and sometimes chaotic environment the art of control is not always about acting but about accepting and encouraging new direction. Karp and Helgo (2007) quote John Maynard Keynes " The greatest difficulty in the world is not for people to accept new ideas, but to make them forget their old ideas" In a sense we should not see control mechanisms as the vehicle for delivery but as away of empowering leadership, "leadership is a process of influencing the patterns of peoples interaction, avoiding design oriented command and control managerial interventions, and keeping at bay the anxiety caused by not being in control" Karp and Helgo (2007)

Older organisations operating a more mechanistic approach to control will need to change to more organic forms of control. While the mechanistic system of "top down" almost dictatorial implementation can function for short periods, especially in a threatening, crisis driven situations. The more organic approach would allow for longer term sustainability. To succeed in organic methods of control it requires a greater resource input in terms of training and communication to be fully embedded within the corporate structure. Which ever method of control is used, for it to be successful there needs to be element of trust between the controlled and the controller.

The supermarket chain Tesco needs to be able to respond to customer requirements rapidly. To enable this to happen the control mechanisms needed to be closer to the customer. In 1997 Terry Leahry took on the post of CEO. He went on to develop the "Steering Wheel" approach to controlling the direction of the company. This is a balanced scorecard quadrant with the company's key performance indicators covering Customer, Operations, People and Finance. The relevant business unit is responsible for delivering on its KPI's. This system gives operational control to the "grass roots" while maintaining the key objectives of the company. Broody (2008).

Striving to deliver key objectives for an organisation with an unmotivated workforce is a contradiction in good strategy. The values individuals place in their personal career and job activities becomes crucial knowledge for the employer. The argument that you get what you pay for is, today, fundamentally wrong. It is based on the concept that money is king. We can see with the structure of modern firms that there are many factors to stimulate worker output, it could be said that "you get what you inspire." Within agency theory there is always the conflict of person and organisation benefit. If a salesman is rewarded for selling product A but not product B, then he will sell A even if B is the better product for the purchaser. The result is that the purchaser will relate the wrong product choice to the organisation and not necessarily the salesman. Direct financial reward, particularly in sales is valid providing the reward is geared to sustainable relationship development. There are flaws in any financially driven model however, as Gibbons(1998) highlights there is a risk that managers may manipulate the timing / invoicing or reporting of events to show a false improvement in performance. It may be as Lazear (1998) quoted in Gibbons (1998) " Weak incentives maybe more efficient than strong but dysfunctional incentives." This is supported By Baker (1992) "it is no use creating strong incentives for wrong actions"

In a more autonomous organisational structure it is proposed by Langfred and Moye (2004) that "The relationship between task autonomy and performance is mediated by motivation such that greater task autonomy leads to higher performance by increasing motivation." This brings us back to the concept of inspiring for profit and not paying for profit. If a worker has value in the work they perform, they can see a positive output and are encouraged, they will strive to achieve more. This could be equated with productivity or skill acquisition. When we look at evaluation of performance within the concept of skill acquisition we need to identify the benefit for the individual and organisation for the implementation of effective reward systems. The investment in employees is a risk and requires a more subjective assessment of the future value of the employees future input to the organisation. To promote / reward on the basis of skill acquisition is only one direction a firm should take. The risk associated with rewarding skill based workers is that it becomes possible for good workers, not undertaking additional training, to be disenfranchised from the reward structure because they do not need to develop additional skills when they are focused on the skill they have that are beneficial to the output of the organisation. As Gibbons (1998) highlights the problem of the "up and out or up and stay" rule the risk is that "firing these wastes their specific capital" Up skilling is a classical way of investing in a workforce for the ultimate benefit of the organisation, however, the risk is that if the motivational factor does not encourage corporate loyalty then the firm exposes itself to losing trained staff to other organisations with perceived better value for the worker.

Having moved from the commercial sector to work for a 'Not for profit' organisation has been a very interesting and challenging experience. Motivation of people who generally are committed to the movement is not a difficult task, the issue is to ensure that they are not de-motivated, a practice that could be utilized in the commercial sector. The organisation I work for is a community radio station, it is managed and operated by a team of volunteers from the community, all with a passion for radio and social inclusion. One of the key roles I play is to ensure that all are heard and have access to skills development. By empowering people within the organisation and valuing their opinion while working towards a single focused objective "Aiming to be a leader in community broadcasting" We retain a high percentage of volunteers and fall out is more to circumstance rather than disapproval of the organisational environment. This is a natural process that really focuses on a minority of influential members, those who are respected by other members. If you keep these people on board and on track then their enthusiasm will help motivate and inspire others. Drucker (1999) re-enforces this by saying that you should aim to keep the top 10% and the rest will follow, if you lose the top 10% the rest also go. The key motivator is ownership. If people have ownership then this inspires and rewards systems are then based on acknowledgement and recognition of work done.

Strategic organisation for innovation and growth

As individual attitudes to work become more complex and the need for a workforce that can adapt and react to hyper competition the new organisation must implement strategies and functional mechanisms that facilitate individual and team innovation while ensuring that strategic routes are maintained.

Innovation through acquisition is one method for an organisation to stay ahead. Forming and operating a proactive policy of acquisition for innovation must be seen in the context of achieving the strategic goals of the organisation. Several technology focused companies have followed this route in the believe that its is the fastest way to competitive advantage. However, there are weaknesses to this policy if it is over used and inefficiently implemented. Stepping out of ones market through perceived innovation and reaction to emerging markets can be a critical mistake for those that innovate for the sake of innovation. Roberts (2004) identifies several examples of organisations innovating through acquisition, a policy that can have short term rewards but also carries inerrant dangers.

While encouraging innovation and alternative approaches that follow the strategic path of the organisation it becomes a vital part of the process to ensure that ideas are turned into reality. Shepherd and Ahmed (2000)   point out that innovation moved from a "market pull" to a "technology push" situation this requires that companies start to drive customer desire for a new "must have" products. They go on to state that "An estimated 40 per cent of sales from US firms came from new products in 1986." With a high dependence on new product development (NPD) the organisational mechanisms needed to capitalize on ideas must reward and encourage even when concepts do not materialize into profitable products or solutions. Child (2005) establishes two stages of innovation - Creative and developmental, although creative environments need a less regimented structure Child (2005) identifies that "Although organisational requirements differ between the two stages of innovation, research suggests that certain more general features are likely to facilitate innovation." It becomes imperative to move through a chain of development, from concept to delivery. This chain needs to be part of the organisation strategical process. The chain or framework for the NPD was suggested by Shepherd and Ahmed (2000), it consisted of 4 key elements:

(1) A senior, cross-functional management team responsible for reviewing programmes and making associated GO/NO-GO decisions.

(2) Empowered cross-functional execution teams who are responsible for an effective execution and management of product development programmes.

(3) Aligned cross-functional processes providing an execution roadmap for all employees and ensuring activities are effectively co-ordinated and aligned.

(4) Specific ``decision points'' or milestones, which demand the delivery of specific deliverables. These are employed to allow the senior cross-functional management team to review programme progress and attractiveness.

Innovating for success and achieving the competitive advantage in the fast moving global economy is a key part of organisational structure. Roberts and Amit (2003) conclude that "a firm's history of innovative activity significantly affects its current financial performance " they were talking in connection with the Australian retail banking system but I believe the statement is true to most successful organisations. To implement successful strategies for innovation it is important to foster a culture that accommodates and encourages tolerance, values ideas no matter how "off the wall" they may be and allows for and accepts failure as part of success.

In the mid 90's I headed a small Internet development company in the UK. We delivered English language lessons online linked to news programmes from BBC, EBN and NBC. This was a fast moving sector and we were always looking for new areas to help deliver our key services. I came across a product that was under development by a company in the US that incorporated a telephone and modem with screen and keyboard that allowed connection to the web. At the time it was the first such smartphone. We secured the UK distribution rights. However, by the time the phone was approved for use on the UK telephone network new and better systems were reaching the market. The phone was called the Cidco iPhone. This demonstrates that there is a risk associated with the acquisition of new technology.

Strategic organisation for performance

Outsourcing

While there are many areas that offer the opportunity for outsourcing I have taken the area of call centre operations as my focus. The issues around call centre activity have been an area of contention within the consumer focused arena for some time. Public faced operations are one of the critical areas of concern for a company. Future business is dictated, in part, by the experience of the customer. It becomes important that organisations control and direct the actions of the public face environment. Outsourcing long term customer care and account management processes to independent call centers requires specific cross organisation communication systems that are open and responsive to customer needs. When Roberts (2004) talks about long term relationships he says " the relative focus for each party is supposed to shift away from appropriating value and towards creating value..." Therefore we see that the development of a symbiotic relationship is going to be more beneficial, the call centre staff have longer to attach themselves to the parent company culture and ethos, along with gaining greater understanding of issues that present and the solutions required. In reality, these relationships are properly too unstable and not sustainable in the long term.

Customer attitudes to call centre managed processes is perceived as unfavorable especially when outsourced to "foreign" companies. Companies within the UK are reacting to this public opinion by actively promoting the fact that their call centers are based in the UK. e.g. Direct Line Insurance and Churchill Insurance. The shortfall in performance or perceived performance may be due to clinical automated responses of centers Customers look for empathy and call centre managers look for reaction time, additional sales and customer turnover. Jaiswal (2008) found that "call centers managers overly depend on metrics comprising operational measures for service quality evaluation. Operational variables cannot provide a true picture of how customers perceive service quality." It is the this mechanical management of call centre that can damage the parent company image and outsourcing customer contact should be done only if the company can establish cross company monitoring and quality service level agreements. While there are significant cost implications for outsourcing call centre operations these must be balanced with customer needs. It is true that a well briefed and educated workforce will go a long way in ensuring that the customers needs are met. Dean (2002) concluded that "Both service quality and perceived customer orientation of call centers affect customer loyalty to the providing organisation"

One area that has developed a prosperous market for outsourced call centre operations is India. With a highly educated workforce and much lower employment cost it has become a strong argument for outsourcing. Several major UK companies have made the move to outsourcing call centre activities to India and as Child (2005) identifies that costs are considerably lower, it is a tempting consideration. The issue is for me not "who and where" the call centre activity happens but "how". The risks associated with outsourcing customer contact can be high. Like all risks associated with agency theory it is paramount that measures of benefit are determined for both parties. The risks of a short-term customer awareness or data collection campaign are far less than the long term customer service contract. Long term outsourcing of key business functions may become less viable if parent companies need to excessively monitor, manage and correct the the activities and practices of the hired company. As Child (2005) cites that in a Dun & Bradstreet survey nearly 70% of companies questioned complained of "failings in supplier competence, poor service, or that costs were too high."This risk is a driving factor for companies to establish call centre management systems within their own organisation.

Technology and a larger call centre aware workforce reduces the once difficult process of establishing in house telephone based service centers

My only experience around call centre operations was based on qualifying sales leads for a project I was hired to develop and implement. We established a small pro-active call team to generate leads internationally. As a way of increasing leads for specific time frame we also outsourced part of the operation. The result was that the external company produced proportionally more leads but with a much lower conversion rate, in fact the entire outsourced activity proved to be significantly more expensive. I would argue that before outsourcing call centre activity a company should evaluate the potential down side of exposing their image and reputation to an outside organisation that may even be operating several contracts. This may be a position that seems to cover all bases but I do believe that there is no golden rule and each case must be assessed on its merits.

Network forms of organisation

With complexities of today's global markets and the increased sophistication of customers, the concept of bonding two or more organisations to ensure the generation or maintenance of competitive advantage is becoming more critical. The more traditional approaches of "go it alone" are becoming more difficult to achieve because of reasons around skills diversification, costs and cultural diversification. By aligning specific objectives it can become advantageous for organisations to embark on partnerships that help further their strategic aims. It could be said that with the increase in potential markets the concept of partnering specialist skills or harmonizing product ranges is a natural development or evolutionary step in the commercial sector.

Strategic alliance is deemed to be a long term partnership in most cases, it is important that both partners are aware of issues or possible events or scenarios that may adversely effect the structural or commercial integrity of the individual companies. Entering into an alliance requires due diligence by both parties to ensure there is a true understanding of cultural, strategic and commercial objectives.

While these strategic partnerships allow for stronger penetration of markets there is always the issue around communication and corporate cultural harmonization It becomes imperative for all parties to define a way and means of communication and reaction processes at all levels of the partnership. The development of the partnership may necessitate the formation of a totally new operating structure in relation to the specific activities of the partnership. This "hybrid organisation" may develop its own culture independently of the parent partners. However, this new structure may be focused to deliver on competitive advantage, at some point there will be issues between the partnership. Mitronen and Moller (2003) highlight four domains of tension in hybrid organisations. These areas of governance, structure and mechanisms, player and activity. one area of tension - governance is "due to contradiction experienced by parties with respect to the governance mechanisms adopted or those that are available" For the formation of the hybrid organisation to withstand the demanding tensions created within the relationship Mitronen and Moller (2003) conclude "In a hybrid organisation, it is necessary to establish and combine well-organized structures, management policies, control and coordination mechanisms of independent flexibility and centralized operations, and the values and norms supporting these."

The concept of strategic partnerships in its many forms as Child (2005) identifies, surrogate subsidiary, balanced partnership, junior partnership and even the development of more independent hybrid organisations is a result of the need for creating solutions for rapid and global growth. In many ways this is a ideal way for organisations to strategically move into new geographical and culturally diverse areas of operation. Also technology development is an area where alliances can benefit parties. We can see that the trend of developmental partnerships at GlaxoSmithKline. 50% of new drugs released by GlaxoSmithKline's would have been developed by external partnerships. It is estimated that between 1/4 and 1/3 of GSK's R&D pipeline will be with external partners. This type of development programme means that by 'virtually' managing partners through its "Centre of Excellence for External Drug Discovery" the company can achieve greater output but reduces risk and costs. Broody (2008)

Which ever route a company takes to make the step into the global environment it will at some point need to look at a partnership arrangement in some form or other. The growing trend towards mutually beneficial alliances means that organisation are facing issues that are fundamental in all human relationships. For them to succeed it is imperative to deal with these issues identified by Child (2005) of trust, conflict resolution and cultural awareness. Once these are addressed then the chances of a successful partnership is more likely.

The environment in which employees work is a reflection of the cultural input of the senior organisation motivators. How the employee responds to the motivation stimuli and implement strategical activity is determined by the process of coordination within that organisation. Forces from markets are drivers only in terms of strategic response function and not directly reward directors. We see that key drivers within the organisations staff can be focused on issues of ownership of ideas, plans and concepts, in fact the whole freedom to innovate scenario. These are drivers that may be instigated by external markets but their creation is based within the comfort of the organisations approach to developing new ideas and concepts. Day and Wendler (1998) point out "In their purest forms, markets emphasize motivation and hierarchies emphasize coordination. Every organizational form falls somewhere between these two extremes, establishing its own trade-off between personal initiative and enforced cooperation"

Generally it can be accepted that the driving factor within an organisation comes from internal activity and direction. The relationship between organisation and employee is a tentative one. Many elements can effect the over all performance and benefit. The employees see the comfort of a bonded relationship with the organisation and the organisation sees benefit in being able to internally coordinate or control the outputs of the worker to achieve the goals of the organisation. If the worker is outside of the organisation then the motivation parameters change and the coordination of the workers activity becomes more difficult.

Coordinating the work force is not just about giving orders and expecting compliance and completion. It is required to inspire ownership of the goal achievement process as Simon (1995) points out "Doing the job well is not mainly a matter of responding to commands, but is much more a matter of taking initiative to advance organizational objectives." It is the role of the organisation to direct and support activities that allow the organisation to reach its objectives through the efforts of its staff.

Identification of processes of coordination and motivation within a corporate or any other organisation is key to successful implementation and fulfillment of defined objectives and the contributors to objective strategy. The proposition of the writers is founded in that it can be identified in organisations functional activity processes. Markets serve to inspire organisations, but it is the organisation that creates the business activity through coordination and motivation of its work force.

There are factors that are capable of motivating and coordinating responses of the employee that do originate within the markets. These motivators are linked to the identification of gaps within the market, identified by the individual, that are beneficial to the identifying individual and not necessarily to the organisation. This type of activity will impact on the actions of other workers within the organisation. The interdependencies that are required within the organisation will suffer as highlighted by Roberts (2004) "Selfish behavior would potentially lead to inefficiencies, because the decision maker takes account of only some costs and benefits of his actions,namely, those he experiences personally"

We can conclude that the propositions of Roberts(2004) and Simon (1995) are valid within the context of contemporary organisational structures. Motivational approaches to organisational development within the markets is a key route to achieving set goals, it is however, the ability to coordinate the activities of the motivated that ensure the success.

Managing organisational change

The nature of change and how we instigate and accommodate its implementation is a fundamental piece of managerial knowledge. Perspectives to change vary from the point of the observer and the introducer. The impression experienced by each audience, individuals, teams, the organisation and external customers, will require different approaches in its introduction.

Understanding the process of change requires the identification of the original driving force origins. These can manifest either externally or internally to the organisation. With the development of the flat more participative organisation the development of change becomes more democratic. Finding solutions to issues that arise can be explored over the whole company to create ownership of change. Child (2005) points out the role of managers "Rather than workout specific solutions at an early stage in the change process, they can encourage new solutions to emerge at lower levels" Coping with and reacting to externally driven change is in many ways easier to deal with for an organisation. Here we see the coming together of organisational teams to face the issues of change and respond in ways that benefit the organisation. In this facing "the enemy" it is easier to motivate staff to accept and implement reactionary change.

With expanding global markets and rapidly changing consumer needs it become more imperative for the organisation to constantly evolve to meet the consumer need. This hyper-competition requires for on going adoption and change within the firm to maintain the competitive advantage. Child (2005) affirms that "Firms facing greater competition and a higher velocity of change in their industries are under pressure to speed up their rate of reorganization" This state of emergent change coupled with the newer organisation structure is an efficient way of reacting and implementing change in a sustainable way.

Within the context of organisational impact we must identify and implement education processes that attach to the context of change. Dealing with change can be a process of dealing with confrontation if the approach is not measured to the target audience. The very nature of facing change in all aspects of life is challenging and resistance invoking. When faced with implementing change within an organisation it is important, no matter where the change originates, to carry the team along. If change is enforced then the solidity of the resulting formation is naturally weak. To create a solid durable structure through change it is imperative to implement by education and acceptance. Communicating change reasoning throughout the organisation plays a vital role in ensuring successful fulfillment of the change. Frahm and Brown (2007) suggest that "those leading emergent change processes need to ensure that employees and managers expectations align with understanding of the change goal, and the accompanying styles of communication." Being able to harmonize the change process leads to greater acceptance and faster less resistant implementation.

Change has always been an exciting environment for me. I have been an instigator of change in several of the companies and organisations I have worked with. It is this process of education and inspiration that drives me. The organisation I work for at the moment is a small volunteer based radio station. There was no formal structure in operation and no understanding of management and governance when I joined. Instead of just introducing processes and procedures by dictate, which would have been faster, it was necessary to develop a range of training/ workshop activities to implement and gain support for the organisations procedural activities. Although this was a fundamental necessity it did require gentle introduction. Change however simple must be viewed as a potential for success or if mismanaged a disaster.

Chapter 2

Marketing Management

As consumers become more aware and sophisticated, the process of marketing needs to evolve and advance in its mechanisms. Broddy (2008) states that " All organisations face the challenge of understanding what customers want, and ensuring they can meet those expectations."The simple concept that the process of marketing is all about strategic placement of advertisements to meet organisational objectives has developed into a more sophisticated mechanism for delivering messages in a more complex way. Thematically the shift in delivery systems means that the critical focus should remain. That is, the organisation goals will remain the same, better sales, greater awareness or some other message, the strategies employed must take into account the increase in consumer awareness. These changes in audience understanding are the driving factors of being able to get the message across. No matter which contemporary approach or view we take to marketing the outcome of the delivery mechanisms remains the same.

With globalization the need to communicate quickly and effectively is more paramount. In the high tech markets the need to establish product first is one of the key drivers. With large budgets and a large experienced marketing team the major players had in the past, the advantage as pointed out by Meldrum (1995) "A further problem, especially for small business, is that large organizations, and/or ones which wield power in an industry, are usually able to exert considerable influence in the setting of standards by having people qualified and available to sit on a standards body, by being able to insist on their inclusion and by being in a better position to influence market perceptions" As a result of competing with the major players campaigns for the small emerging companies there was a need to develop new fast traveling low cost ways of communicating messages. This resulted in the pro-active use of the internet. On-line marketing ,social networks and viral campaigns have played a critical part in launching new products to a global market. Ramirez (n.d) points out that "Online social networking and social media marketing are an amazingly cost effect means of spreading the brand message and building both customer rapport and loyalty." These new methods of marketing have been so successful that large international organisations are now employing these techniques.

We can see the shift in delivery methods of messages within the "not for profit" sector. Over the past few years we have seen charitable organisations adopt and adapt marketing strategies to increase awareness of issues and enhance fund raising activities. This has been a difficult process but one that has paid off. Two areas that are contentious are direct mail and legacy campaigns. It was only because of the success of these new ways that the professionalisation of "not for profit" sector marketing and promotion activities is becoming more acceptable. The emergence of relationship marketing plays a new and valuable role in promoting and developing the aims and objective of many "not for profit" organisations. During the mid nineties I worked for the fund raising dept. of the British Red Cross. At this time the organisation was undergoing radical change and there was a major cultural change within the marketing and fund raising depts. One of the key marketing objectives was to communicate to the membership the need to employ more commercially based marketing practices for the benefit of the organisation.

Understanding and accepting that customers are more aware and in tune with marketing techniques is a theme that purveys through the development of marketing strategies in today's globalization of markets.

Conceptual framework of market orientation

Marketing trends and strategies designed to capture audience participation in an organisations goals that focus on the conceptual framework of 5 emerging principles identified by Lafferty and Hult (1999). Based on market orientation the principles allow for a framework that permits the development of strategies that meet the goals of the organisation while working on the premiss that customer values and wants drive the organisational goals. By focusing on the customer it has become vital for organisation staff to "buy in" and have ownership of the identified values and the mechanisms employed to implement the strategy. By embedding the principles of market orientation throughout the organisation the staff are able to remain on board and on message. we shall look at the emerging principles and assess the described frameworks and the applications within current organisational activities.

Hyper-competition is driving rapid an revolutionary changes in the way organisation innovate and capture competitive advantage. By covering the needs of the customer and counter-balancing the activities of competitors the organisation can enhance and develop the distribution of its message and brand. Reviewing Lafferty and Hult (1999) perspective of the following market orientated activities, (1) the decision-making perspective; (2) the market intelligence perspective; (3) the culturally based behavioral perspective; (4) the strategic perspective; and (5) the customer perspective, we can begin to account for there impact and effectiveness within today's markets.

The decision-making perspective.

In line with the general trend of organisational structure, the policy of cross organisational communication is a fundamental. By instilling and exploring customer and market trends and needs from distant and internal information sources the collective can calculate and react to market needs in an innovative fashion.

The market intelligence perspective.

Information gathering is the key to developing effective and clear messages. One of the skills maximized within this perspective would be the ability to identify future trends. As Kohli and Jaworski (1990) cited by Lafferty and Hult (1999) identify the assimilation of information from many integrated and independent sources are required. This information should be delivered and responded to in a inter-organisational manner.

The culturally based behavioral perspective.

Understanding the customer in an global market is a multi tasked approach. Accepting and incorporating mechanisms that account for and adapt to differences in cultural perspectives, understanding and activity are key processes of activating successful campaigns. The same could be said of an organisations competitors as well as identifying weak areas that can be targeted for competitive advantage. The information gleamed from identifying activities must be distributed and acted upon on an organisational wide basis.

The strategic perspective.

The use of information and the empowerment of managers to collect and act on information in a strategic sense is a critical part of an organisations ability to develop and satisfy consumer need. By identifying needs of customers we can manipulate strategies around organisational goals to accommodate the customers perceived need and deliver on internally driven aims.

The customer perspective.

Focusing on the customer in a singular manner is a cultural approach that may be best suited in areas that demand high customer value and internal or external market domination in niche markets. Otherwise solely focusing on the customer may critically damage internal innovation and growth potential through lack of competition knowledge and positioning.

As Lafferty and Hult (1999) identify "Three of the five models indicate the need for the organization to generate and utilize information on competitors as well." This indicates that there is a growing understanding for the needs of the customer through the delivery mechanisms and strategies of the competitor. The customer and competitor are intrinsically joined as defined by Sørensen (2008) "Customer orientation and competitor orientation are each defined symmetrically to market orientation, incorporating the components of generation and dissemination of intelligence and action." This trend of interdependence within organisational structure is symptomatic of the changes within organisational structure in a hyper-competitive environment, more free flowing information and innovative means of implementing strategies that are formed by the dissemination of information have become a cultural part of all departments within organisations.

When we look at the effects on the profitability of market orientation through customer value, transference of information and the strategic delivery of corporate and sales messages we can see that it plays an important part in reaching a level of understanding with the customer. The impact of market orientation within companies was highlighted by Lancaster (2004) "results in business performance make it worthwhile to implement market orientation programmes." In conclusion we can see that the future of organisations will rely on its understanding the direction and needs of its existing and future customers, market orientation is a key driver in meeting these needs.

Decision Making

The process of embarking on a family visit to a restaurant requires both collective and individual decision processes. For a decision to be made there needs to be at least two options available for a decision to be made. We will explore the activities undertaken to decide a venue and the information available and its use in attaining a consensus. There will also be decisions made on an individual bases that may or may not impact on other individuals within the group. Kacem & Lee (2002) "The tendency to focus on group preferences and group harmony in collectivist cultures leads to an ability to repress internal (personal) attributes in certain settings. Accordingly, people in collectivist cultures often shift their behavior de-pending on the context or what is "right" for the situation". Factors that impact on an activity of this nature would involve identifying an environment that is conducive to the majority of the group. How we attribute or perceive an establishment, the activities used by the venue to attract customers and how that meets the needs of the group/consumer, influence the final decision.

The fundamental activities of establishments in reaching and persuading potential customers to frequent their venue will play a significant part in the groups decision making. Each member may attribute that information in a way that meets their own individual views and perspectives. The attraction of a fast food outlet may attract children with free gifts with food, the parents may see this as unhealthy food but would be willing to patronize the establishment to please the children against their better judgement . One could say that the comments of Linn (2004) "Given the intensity and pervasiveness of marketing to children, it is either cynical or naive to assume that individual parents should bear the sole burden of shielding children from the potentially harmful effects of a $15 billion industry." are an escape for parents in a high pressure consumerist approach to food. Decision making against sophisticated marketing will require objective criteria establishment, something that can be difficult so alternatives can be presented that may deflect from the influences of the larger food chains.

In conclusion we can see that the influences on families when going for a nice family visit to a restaurant release a wide range of commercial influences, free gifts, low prices and established character figures. While we may attribute a specific culture to the organisation we can also be impacted by the type of food available. This is becoming more important as we identify with "healthy choices" so much so that the issue is being addressed by fast food chains and used to influence parents as a method of counter pointing established view points. As a parent I wish to provide my children with healthy food in a fun environment, while I have doubts about the fast food chains I can see that they have identified this general concern and are addressing it in the promotion of their product. Marketing through education is proving a strong influence, this dissemination of information is identified by Mizeski et al (1979) "An information source could affect the stability of consumer's attribution through the consistency dimension by providing education or instruction." Identifying the spin and the education of food marketing is a difficult process that requires expert understanding and evaluation, a resource not available to most consumers.

A Date with Data

We meet with data collectors on a daily basis and the general view is that its a part of a modern day life or at least something that we should accept. However, there appears to be an increase in consumer awareness in connection with data collection and growing concerns of invasions of privacy and risk of identity theft. One of the driving factors of this awareness today is in the emergence of identity theft, in particular when it concerns finance. Looking at two particular arrears of data collection and action monitoring, loyalty cards and on-line shopping, we will examine changing approaches by the consumer. While Graeff,& Harmon (2002) addressed a growing concern about the use of personal data and monitoring of individuals purchasing actions, even though concerns were highlighted, there was a degree of acceptance by the consumer. This growing awareness may not change purchasing habits with established organisations but will make consumers more sensitive to providing data to unknown bodies.

Graeff,& Harmon (2002) said that "Just because a consumer is concerned about how their personal information is collected and used does not mean that he or she will reduce their amount of purchasing." However since 2002 there has been increased awareness around data collection, at one of the UKs leading retailers and operator of a loyalty card scheme,Tesco, Humby (2004) identified that "One of the consistent problems with loyalty programmes is that while customers are enthusiastic about participation in the process, when confronted with the volume of data that the company running the scheme has collected, they are less comfortable." Loyalty cards still play a major part in the Tesco marketing strategy and will continue to do so as long as the public are willing to continue to 'sell' information to them. Issues around privacy do not come into play because the individual is not forced to participate in the 'selling' of their information.

With increases in on-line shopping since 2002 we can see that consumers are more willing to give information about themselves and their financial information. This may be due to the efforts of banks and organisations, like PayPal, that have established secure methods of collecting information. Even with this increase in confidence or willingness to participate in transactions on-line Listerman & Romesberg (2009) highlight that "the rate of data breach incidents has risen more than 400% since 2005" in connection with on-line identity theft.

When we look at the issues around gender and demographics in parting with information there seems to be a variance in who is more concerned. Graeff,& Harmon (2002) indicated that males were less concerned about privacy issues and how the information maybe used although higher income individuals were more likely to want to now what the information would be used for. Although Park (2008) found that "Gender did not play a significant role for the respondents' beliefs in on-line privacy rights" As the consumer becomes more aware of the issues and hazards of providing information then any demographic differences in attitude will dilute, as seen with the time difference, six years, of two papers quoted here.

The practice of collecting, selling and using of data collected from consumers will continue to play an ever increasing role in the marketing activities of organisations. There will be a need to reassure consumers that the information they provide will be safe and only used for agreed purposes. The data protection laws enacted in the UK and other countries go some way to protecting the individual from legitimate traders in data. A higher awareness of how and when the individual delivers data will play a major role in determining the collection processes of the future, already we can see on-line activity that encourages individuals to 'sell' personal information for points, samples or even cash rewards. Our date with data will flourish into a long term relationship that will impact on all aspects of our lives.

Product Development

Producing a limited range of product that satisfies consumer need and establishes brand identity is an effective way of sustaining an organisations market development. The ability to identify specific customer groups is key to product development and introduction. This segmentation can be affected by both geographic and socio-economic variables and organisations should modify marketing activity to account for this. However, we should recognise that the development of production systems means that there can be variations in final product format. This variation can give the perception of a wide range of products but is in fact just a process of construction of added value packaging.

Although the approach of a few general products targeted at 'Mr average consumer' could be seen as a safe way to capture market share, we must be aware of the faster moving and changing attitudes to product development by consumers. In particular in the technology sector, which as a hungry consumer base, needs to segment its market in numerous ways to continue to sell. While the basics of computer hardware remain the same,the targeting of niche markets within the segmented audience is a critical part of successful sales. The segmentation of the PC market has moved to mass customization with Dell among others allowing consumers to design and customize the PC they feel they need. This, Kara & Kaynak (1996) 'finer segmentation' could be seen as the way forward. With technological and production advances the concept of mass customization is going to play a larger part of global organisation strategies. Kara & Kaynak (1997) "the number, variety and assortment of products manufactured will be substantially higher than that available under traditional segmentation"

Organizations face the dilemma of focusing on mass customization or limiting potential growth by focusing on more traditional segmentation, even niche areas could become vulnerable if attention is not paid to a growing desire by the consumer for more personalization of products and services. There will be a growing move towards creating mass customization in areas that have traditionally focused on either mass production or output focused on broad area of segmentation, either cultural, geographic or socio-economic. The future is for the individual. Although Fogliatto & Silveira (2008) state that "At the operational level, process flexibility capabilities should correspond to those products and features being most valued by customers." we will see marketing activities in a wide range of markets directing consumers to a perceived individualization of product, creating a uniqueness to ownership. This means that as Kotler &Keller (2009) identify "..the key is adjusting the marketing program to recognize customer differences"

We can see that segmentation plays an important part in the profitably of an organisation, but that segmentation needs to evolve into mass customization as the more discerning consumer opens up to more flexible and specific product needs. How organisation strategically embark on this will be to some extent be determined by their industry and the consumer profile and as Kara & Kaynak (1997) say "it is generally recognized that there is no one best way to segment markets, as each approach has certain merits and limitations". As their is no best way then the opportunity for innovation is very prominent and vital for the expansion and enhancement of the consumer sector. The future of profitability is in the identification of, and the desire generation in the individual customer to have a product made for them. This mass customization is an extension of Henry Fords objective of supplying "one for all". With the new technology in production and delivery systems the 'one for all' is still a very potent sales pitch, only today it means a unique product not a mass produced one.

Lifestyle and the travelers dream: The future of tourism.

Looking at the development of the tourist industry over recent years and how trends determine choices and how changes in lifestyle and economic prosperity influence consumer choice is a crucial mechanism in developing new and innovative holiday choices. The influence of lifestyles and the simplifying of travel opportunities has given the tourist industry a strong growth, even in times of economic difficulty the trend towards rest and relaxation is still high on the individuals agenda. The influences that determine choices of destination and activity are linked to the aspirations of the consumer. To meet the needs of these consumers marketeers are embarking on greater segmentation to facilitate the demands of a consumer who is more aware, better educated and less afraid of new destinations than the early days of package travel.

To better understand the full potential of market share, organisations are moving towards greater segmentation of it customer base. This segmentation as been noted on a basic level for most tourism stakeholders by Tkacynski et al (2008) that "Most tourism stakeholders profile their tourists using between two and four segmentation bases. The most common variables used to profile tourists were activities sought (behavioral), location (geographic), income (demographic), trip purpose and motivations (psychographic)." However, in light of greater choice for the consumer this over simplified approach may be derogatory to the aims of the tour operator. The upturn in self arranged holidays means that tour operators need to source more exotic or special interest holidays out of reach of the average tourist. This requires greater understanding of drivers in lifestyle and 'dream-style' environments of the potential customer. In their research Gonzalez & Bello (2002) segmented the market "into five clusters: home-loving, idealistic, independent, hedonistic and conservative." The needs of the customer may well be based on a hierarchy of travel motives as highlighted by Gonzalez & Bello (2002). These motivators are becoming more sophisticated and demanding no matter which area of segmentation we look at. In the past holidays were an opportunity to withdrawn from everyday life. Now holidays are about enhancing our lifestyles. This as resulted in a more diverse and complicated approach to capturing market share. Tkacynski et al (2008) "Today's tourism marketers must influence consumer decision making in an increasingly complex and competitive global marketplace."

There are now many factors that determine the choice of the consumer that fall outside the normal destination- activity sphere. Pan et al (2009) "Tourism is a combination of many sectors that, in turn, influence and are influenced by other sectors." The external influences today include fears of terrorism and pandemic, these fears must be addressed by marketeers and governments to ensure the sustainability of the industry. The consumers desire to use the holiday as an extension of their lifestyle is highlighted by Pan et al (2009) "Travel has become more activity-interest based" The focus on lifestyle segmentation by marketeers will out of necessity become more integrated in the lifestyle of consumers.

Gonzalez & Bello (2002) have laid the path for understanding the choices being made by a knowledge rich audience. Alternative approaches to tourism should now be seen as the normal approach. The growing sophistication and finer segmentation of market audiences will ensure that customized holidays remain high on the agenda of tour operators. The success will be in identifying efficiently the segmentation trends and communicating availability without moving away from the consumers lifestyle.

Is PLC PC?

The role of marketing within and in relation to the product life-cycle (PLC) is a symbiotic relationship covering all stages, Introduction, Growth, Maturity and Decline. Each area requires a specific action or actions from the marketing team. It will be important that the marketing team monitor and evaluate the activity of the product within its different stages of the cycle. Being able to process the flow of the product will enable the seamless introduction of new product at the end of the cycle. Understanding this cycle and its role is a crucial element for product development and advancement. There is an issue with whether PLC is a reliable measure of the life of a product and that it could be a way of dictating the demise of a product.

It is important to be able to place the product at a particular point at any given time to allow for future planning and development. This could be a difficult task as highlighted by Dhalla Yuspeh (1976) as cited by Grantham (1997) "..it is possible to assume a product is at a particular phase when the opposite may in fact be the case." Miss placing a product within the cycle could have a negative impact in terms of future product introduction, profitability and brand awareness. There is also a risk that the product could be undervalued within its market because of the drive to introduce new product. This need to rapidly develop may lead to organisation shortening the life-cycle of a product in favour of a newer shiner successor. Placing too much focus on a theoretical process runs the risk of the product not having its full potential fully realized even if re-branding or re packaging may be required towards the end of the process. The marketing team should play a significant role to ensure that potential of a product is achieved and deter their organisation from over introducing new product while there is still life and profit in the existing model, whether re-packaged or re-branded. There is also a risk that the natural positioning of the product could be missed by theoretical marketing strategies and programmes. Creativity and innovation should be employed to introduce and sustain a product. Marketeers should look at the whole picture and not focus on pre-designed delivery mechanisms, there will be times when the PLC model will fit the product, but it should be viewed as a strategy option only.

With certain products the life cycle is not the 'product' but its target audience. Products that are targeted toward specific evolving targets like an age based groups then the PLC takes on a different momentum requiring the management of all for stages at once as the consumer migrates through the stages associated with this reverse PLC. The product may require re-packaging to ensure it is relevant to current thinking and trends. This scenario is high-lighted by Broody (2008) with the case of Lynx deodorant which targets 15 - 24 year males and therefore needs to introduce and recruit a new customer base of 15 -19 year olds. This type of market means that the product can reach maturity and avoid or significantly delay the onset of decline.

Marketing should not be seen as a reaction to PLC but as an intrinsic part of the entire life-cycle, however, because there is the chance that by following a PLC path it will result in a self fulfilling road to being discontinued. Kotler & Keller (2009) "the PLC pattern is the self-fulfilling result of marketing strategies and that skillful marketing can in fact lead to continued growth." Marketing teams must have a broader view of the market and the consumer.

Brand Space - Getting the bigger picture.

With globalization and the development of rapid information transmission systems the role of the brand manager is becoming a more complex. Understanding the position of the brand and its impact on the consumer will allow greater opportunity for brand sustainability. Taking the brand identity and communicating messages around that brand at different phases of it customer relationship requires the brand manager to identify with the needs of the consumer and the organisation.

Understanding the complexities of a brands status and functionality in the market within the framework of "abstraction and enactment" as defined by Berthon et al (2003) allows for more analytical approach to future development and sustainability of the brand. Identification of this 'Brand Space' outlined by Berthon et al (2003) as four quadrants defined by two axes that allows the brand manager the mechanism for placing and managing a brands development. This framework defines the current position of a brand and will allow for a more targeted approach to keeping the brand on message through consumer understanding. The methods of evaluating a brands position and the issues of reassigning a brand image were faced by Berthon et al (2003) who recognized that "many firms have faltered badly in their attempts to extend their brands by moving them into different product categories," Failure to keep the identity or associations of a brand will lead to the potential failure of its linked products as Berthon et al (2003) point out "perceptions of a brand arise from information they receive about it from the company, other customers and third parties"

The application of the Brand Space framework is a useful mechanism for reviewing and managing the complexity of brand positioning and new product vs new brand introduction in global, multi-cultural environment. An organisations lack of understanding of its brand, and the equity in that brand, as on occasions led to new product ranges not naturally associated with the original branded product to fail, while product extension is likely to be more successful Ambler & Styles (1996) cited Sullivan (1992) "…the probability of a brand extension surviving more than six years could be as high as 93 per cent when the extension is launched into a mature market, as opposed to 75 per cent for new brands…" the development of new product ranges is not as likely to capture the heart of the consumer unless the brand as a high abstraction value. We can see the development of the Virgin brand as being able to cross consumer barriers from a Cola to Space Travel. Although the issue of Virgins brand could be questioned in regard to its equity because of the personality association with Richard Branson, the equity may well be in Branson. Brand identity is a sensitive matter and can be damaged by miss association or through association with negative historical actions, e.g. Exxon, and the pollution of the Alaskan coastline and Nestle and the baby formula issue. Nestles programme of providing free formula milk to mothers in developing countries resulted in a worldwide boycott of their products. What was perceived as a positive action in fact became a negative because of the perception that Nestle were exploiting mothers in poverty. Personality association with brand management and development is a risky bond and requires careful management. Entire organisations can be damaged if the associated individual is exposed for some wrong doing e.g. Martha Stewart.. As brands are linked to non product activity through sponsorship of events as a way of linking brand with an ideal or value they run the risk of exposing the brand to negative association. Association with sport for example could adversely effect a brand if that sport or an individual are identified as cheating or using drugs. Failure to maintain emotional and historical value in a brand is becoming a greater risk for brand managers as the information and mis-information world plays a growing role in dissemination of opinion.

Not understanding where the brand fits in the 'brand space quadrant' could seriously impact on the the market development and consumer perception. Critical assessment of non brand space issues should also be accounted for when implementing brand awareness, growth and development. Brand managers must understand the personality of the brand and how it interacts with the consumer. Errors of not connecting brand with the emotional ties of the consumer can lead to a movement away from the brand or as in the "New Coke" case a consumer rebellion and product U-turn as highlighted by Berthon et al (2003). Managers should recognise that brand development is an evolutionary process and will need to assign its development in incremental stages taking into account the attachment by the consumer to the historical context of the brand. We can conclude that the 'brand space' framework can play a role in placing and communicating brand image and message, but only when there is full understanding of the total organisational and consumer environment.

Picking the Price

Price should be seen as a way of communicating with the customer. The factors involved in establishing that price are the determiners for success. A consumer should identify a perceived value to trigger a purchasing action. For the price to be right the marketing manager should evaluate a range of factors both internally and externally to the organisation. There seems to be a trend in not reviewing in depth the issues around pricing. The majority of organisations seem to focus on a 'cost plus' system modified to market trends. While the control of price can be determined by effective management of production and material costs, the service industries need to assess more closely the activity costs associated with the service delivery. Specialist technology based products need careful strategic processes to enable effective, valued placing in the market. Novelty and technological advancement can play a major role in assigning a need value and premium price allocation.

A critical mistake that can be made by organisations is to avoid looking at other strategic issues when setting a price. By focusing on a policy of cost plus decisions a company can miss opportunity to maximise on profit and market development. Avlonitis & Indounas, (2005) "a clear implication for managers responsible for pricing decisions within their firms is to move away from these simplistic cost-plus formulas and treat pricing from a customer's point of view in all the steps of their pricing process."

When reviewing the pricing structure for a new innovative technological product a strategy of developing a 'must have' profile will help to maximise price and recoup high R&D outlay.

Using a high entry price can be risky but it is a strategy employed by many high technological companies including Sony as identified by Kotler & Keller (2009). Apart from the costs associated with the Research and Development of the product there will be issues around the production costs and volume attribution. Once the factors around development and production are accounted then issues around customer value perception come into play. The development of a product profile linked to the Brand is a key element of internal price development influences. Zeithaml (1988) " price is but one of several potentially useful extrinsic cues; brand name or package may be equally or more important "

This can be seen with Apples introduction of the iPhone. "Apple's pricing strategies include setting the price high at the start of launching a new product" Sliwinska et Al (2008). The internal driver to reclaim the expenditure associated with the R&D plays a significant part in Apples introduction pricing policy. However, in terms of prestige the high introduction price increases the perceived value and need of the product, buy also limiting availability of the iPhone Apple added to the 'must have' effect. Apple have avoided the 'cost plus' approach in determining the setting of the introductory price of the iPhone by linking price to the internal strategic and brand marketing policies of the organisation. 'Cost Plus' pricing and going rate pricing strategies will come into play as competitors introduce new products that compete with the trend setting product. This can be seen with the introduction of the second generation iPhone 3G.

When introducing new ground breaking technology it is important to position the products price by taking into account factors such as generating high value and need in the eyes of the customer. This will allow for the development of a larger market at later stages of production or introduction of a Mk2 product. The price of a product has the power to communicate many messages including uniqueness, value, brand identity and desirability. Reviewing all the internal corporate drivers like brand image, marketing strategy, corporate profile, production/distribution and R&D will all contribute to setting the right price.

Delivering the goods

How organisations get their products to the customer in a global market requires the organisation to assess the ways in which it facilitates the delivery of the product to the final consumer. Where timing and availability are key to the distribution of a product, the producing company must measure the resources available internally, and the external impactors, for smooth delivery to the final destination. Successful resource efficient delivery in a fast moving market is a step toward competitive advantage. It is because of changing environment that the view of, and practicalities of, distribution systems are evolving to accommodate global and localised supply chain networks.

For organisations to ensure they produce and deliver products to the consumer in the most efficient and profitable manner they need to remain in control of the entire supply chain. Conventional methods of distribution through independent agents means there is a greater risk of breaks in the supply chain. As each member of the chain is driven by their own goals and objectives there could be the opportunity for conflict of interest and lack of motivation to meet the needs of the producer and the consumer. By taking control of all parts the the supply chain an organisation can more realistically control the output of those parts. However, one could argue that because there are different skill requirements within the various elements of the chain the diversification from producer to wholesaler, distributor and retailer could dilute the operational efficiency of the organisation. Also it maybe that, as identified by Wuyts et al (2004) that "buyers value a sequence of strong ties that run from suppliers through the vendor to the buyer " This can only increase the motivation of organisations to acquire the skill sets needed to gain greater control over the supply chain.

The need to compete competitively and profitably means that organisations need to look at all the mechanisms employed to deliver product to the consumer. By making the channel to the customer more transparent and controllable organisations are taking on more diverse activities and actions to achieve competitive advantage. Satellite television broadcaster Sky recently acquired the independent developer/manufacturer of their set top box, Amstrad. This acquisition meant that Sky would have total control of the development and output of the production process, more enabling them to meet the growing needs of the market. Speaking to the BBC chief executive James Murdoch(2007) said."It will help us to drive innovation and efficiency for the benefit of our customers," Sky also added that "the deal would "significantly" reduce costs in its supply chain"

The movement into controllable delivery systems is going to be a critical element in most organisations development in the future. Whether this movement from the conventional marketing channels to one of the Vertical Marketing Systems (VMS) is through Corporate VMS, Administered VMS or Contractual VMS it does mean that organisations will require more influence and control of the supply chain, dependent on their resource availability. Frazier (1999) "As the world economy evolves, more and more companies are highlighting channel management as among their very top priorities"

Advertising Problems

Entering new geographic markets for a US pharmaceutical company can pose many issues, in particular how to communicate the benefits of a product or brand of specific drugs to the consumer and dispenser. The many issues including cultural attitudes, consumer influence and legal restrictions will mean that the marketing strategy would need to be adapted from that of the companies home market. Within the The United States there is a driving movement to promote specific drugs directly to the consumer, with the under lying, or in some cases not so underlying message to get the consumer to ask their doctor to prescribe a specific branded drug. There are within the US three activities of communication for pharmaceutical companies.

1. Direct to Consumer Advertising: incorporating multi media distribution of information specifically targeted to public mass audiences, including TV, Radio and Print.

2. Detailing: This is the direct one to one or seminar approach of disseminating information and directing doctors to prescribe specific brands of drugs to their patients or drug purchasing departments of hospitals.

3.Other Marketing Efforts: The use of specialist Print and other technology based delivery methods targeted at professionals within the prescribing sector.

To enter the European market it will a requirement to adjust campaigns to meet legal requirements and restrictions. While in the US DTC is used to promote prescription drugs it is not currently permitted within Europe, although non prescription drugs may be advertised to the consumer. It become necessary to refocus efforts within Europe. There is an EU commission proposal Article 88a of Directive 2004/27/EC to allow the dissemination of information to the consumer via the internet as pointed out by Parmar (2009).

With restrictions on DTC for their prescription drugs companies would need to focus on the "detailing "element of encouraging doctors to prescribe and hospital drug purchasers to stock their drugs.

There would also be an increase needed in trade and professional print advertising to help offset the lack of consumer knowledge regarding drug availability.

To implement drug education with the consumer is a more complex matter outside of the USA and may be better for the consumer in relation to the need and perceived need for specific treatment.

This lack of consumer knowledge may be a positive in respect of a prescriber because they are not put under pressure to prescribe inappropriate drugs. Although the view from the industry is different Parmar (2005) argues that "DTCA provides a favorable environment for shared decision-making wherein the patient is aware of the risks and benefits of new drugs". Berndt E.R (2005) highlights the issue of persuasion "Many of these advertisements do more than simply inform consumers about the availability of a drug; they also attempt to persuade consumers to use it"

No matter the view or interpretation of the issues the company must operate within the law and that means where DTCA is prohibited the focus of promotion must fall to Detailing in the main, supported with other marketing efforts within the trade and professional media.

Detailing and OME are the accepted methods within the more regulated markets of Europe and Asia and they must become the driving arrears for a US pharmaceutical company's inroad into their new marketing areas.

With DTCA has a growing possibility of introduction within Europe and Asia, Taylor and Raymond (2000)"With the continued economic liberalization of Taiwan, PRC, and Korea and the strength of the Japanese market, many more changes in the advertising industry are expected." and while there is potential for greater consumer awareness, the argument for DTCA from the industry, it is important from a consumer perspective to be aware that heath issues are diverse, complicated and driven by the individuals non medical knowledge.

Implementing Marketing

Success for an organisation is dependent on its ability to communicate a broad range of messages to its customers, suppliers and staff. The art of marketing over the last 30 years has seen a tremendous change in mindset and delivery mechanisms. While traditional approaches have been focused on sales objectives, today we see a more holistic approach . The need to convey specific messages externally and internally to assist in the achievement of organisational goals require marketing teams to implement, monitor and react to campaigns. In a global market the position of competitive advantage is in most cases vulnerable to challenges and hence requires adaptive and responsive actions through marketing channels. Failure to act out the delivery systems of a marketing plan and then monitor and accommodate necessary changes will lead to positional and market loss. Modern marketing is a multi-disciplinary act operated through diversified delivery systems.

Theoretical approaches to marketing and the development of marketing plans may look good in the boardroom but if the motivation to implement, deliver and pro-actively monitor the plan is lacking then it is set up to fail. The motivation of organisations to take on marketing activities on an inter-departmental level requires that systems of efficient communication are established as identified by Ryals & Knox (2001) change in working practices so that information is shared between departments to build up a picture of the firm's total relationship with the customer. Effective actioning of a marketing plan will need to be monitored and adapted through time. This monitoring is dependent on Motivation, Opportunity and Ability to process measurement data as identified by Clark et al (2005). The desire by an organisation to follow through its plan should be a major priority. Having established within the organisation the status of the plan it should then establish mechanisms to react to incoming data. This will help ensure functional success of the marketing plan.

Flexibility and responsive marketing plans in a fast moving and expanding environment become the key to successful fulfillment of marketing objectives. Plans that are comprehensive and regimented and fixed do not allow for adaptation within fluctuating markets. Slotegraaf and Dickson(2004)" marketing plans that are comprehensive may inherently produce rigidity effects".

This rigidity is going to result in unresponsive and non adaptive actions that could lead to market loss or lack of understanding of internal and external messages.

How organisations succeed in their marketing highlights how poor implementation will lead to reduced output, lower sales and poor brand recognition. Maintaining control of an integrated marketing plan is one of the keys to global success. Manchester United football club is a good example of how controlling the marketing strategy and internal implementation of the marketing plan can lead to one of the strongest global sporting brands. This strategy of total control based on the success of the team and the individual personalities linked to the club results in MU being a major brand around the world. Broody (2008) states that "The management believes this enhances the ability to deliver branded services to customers any where in the world" Failure to identify and react to the marketing plan would result in poorer recognition and branded sales.

Functional application of a responsive holistic marketing plan is a critical part of an organisations fundamental make up. The marketing plan is not a paper exercise but a fully functioning organic process within a cross departmental system of multi channel communications.

Chapter 3

International Business and Emerging Markets

The international business environment

Globalization Development

The delivery of the globalization dream is full of conflicting concepts and political exploitation. International commercial interests in terms of market penetration and competitive advantage development are influenced in outcome by not only commercial decisions but political manipulation and in some cases corruption. To say that globalization is a route out of poverty for developing countries could be argued on a very basic level, however, commercially driven strategies where profit is king will lead to exploitation and manipulation of the poor and disenfranchised in the developing countries. The utopian believe that global free trade will lead to greater wealth distribution and high living standards is lost and unachievable while political interference and exploitation prevail. We can see examples of states enhancing their development within Europe e.g Spain and Ireland mostly generated by political will, economic enhancements and infrastructure subsidies from the EU rather than pure commercial sense and resource availability in a free trade environment. These advantages of commercial incentives and infrastructure subsidies are not so available to third world developing countries. In the areas of manufacturing the opportunity for exploitation in developing countries is greatest, and, we have seen this with the exposure of several western brands use of sweatshops and child exploitation.

Taking on board the pitfalls and exploitative potential of globalization it is important to recognise and develop the advantages that can become available for all organisations, countries and individuals. We are all in an interconnected world and with the ever increasing rates of technological expansion the opportunity to integrate culturally and commercially sensitive organisational expansion is key to overcoming poverty and allowing individual enhancement. With globalization comes social and cultural responsibility.

Recent examples of rapid growth in developing countries are now being exposed to rapid decline because the bases of growth was exploitation and not sustainable development. For globalization to succeed in developing countries it must focus on sustainable development. The full implementation of a free global economy must be developed on commercial equality and not inequality, although Lindert and Williamson (2001) argue "the source of that inequality would be poor government and non-democracy in those lagging countries, not globalization" This may be true but business and politics, hence governments, exist and operate in unison. Although Cook and Kirkpatrick (1995) point out "there continues to be a general skepticism regarding the capacity of government to intervene in a manner that will improve overall well-being."

Examples of successful integration by organisations can in fact be misleading if we look at the city of Bangalore in India, a city perceived as a modern thriving environment built on the establishment of international technology companies. Madon (1997) highlights several issues of concern around the internationalization of employment including rampant wage increases, infrastructure deficiencies including power shortages as the city tries to deal with rapid expansion. While we can see elements of benefit in the establishment of new business in poor undeveloped areas it must be understood that if the wealth generation is not channelled in to social development and gain then the divergence between rich and poor will grow and conflict and instability will ensue.

Technological development is a good example of injecting economic growth in to an area but as Madon (1997) highlights "There is an evident tension between the notions of entering the global information society and local development." For successful globalization we must look further than the balance sheet and look in to effecting sustainable social gain and cultural integration.

New Ventures

Globalised economy structures and the freeing up of currency restrictions is an ideal environment for the establishment of INV's for new and emerging organisations. The very nature of small start up operations, innovative adaptability and market penetration flexibility are best suited to creating competitive advantage globally. Traditional established organisations expanding into new international ventures face more implementation issues such as organisational cultural trends and restrictive internal bureaucratic practices that may be unable to adapt to new market cultures.

To successfully establish an INV there are several elements and criteria that have been identified as being key factors, entrepreneurship, resourcefulness and adaptability. These factors have been evaluated and established as fundamentals to success. While these established fundamentals are recognized it is also an important part of project criteria to highlight that the concept of organisational structural fluidity to meet the specific requirements of the operating environment. A system more appropriate to young emerging organisations than established leviathans.

New technological advances have created opportunity for young and new organisations to penetrate larger global markets. As Oviatt & McDougall (1993) highlight global start ups may be more difficult than domestic based, although they do seem to show a more sustainable market position. With new operations the impact of little resource availability means the outsourcing of services specific to the cultural and social environments add to the customization of market penetration and allows for faster competitive advantage to be established. This was identified by Oviatt & McDougall (1993)

Oviatt & McDougall (1994) lay down the theories of INV which have the bases for successful integration for new ventures in an international context. When identifying attributes for success they highlight resourcefulness and entrepreneurship as key elements. These elements will allow young vibrant companies to assimilate and expand in diverse cultural markets. Unlike large top heavy corporations entering a new international arena. In fact as Oviatt & McDougall (1994) state the size of the organisation is not the focus but the age. Newer fresher organisations focusing specifically on entering the international arena are more capable of achieving competitive advantage because of their evolutionary and adaptable approaches.

When entering new markets on an international level it is vital to maintain control and monitor activities in a variance of marketplaces. This concept was pointed out by Oviatt & McDougall (1994) "Their emphasis on controlling rather than owning assets is due to resource scarcity that is common among new organizations." This ability to establish non owned assets and resources while imposing control is a critical force in developing and maintaining competitive advantage. Organizations that fit and apply the principles of entrepreneurship and resourcefulness will find a smoother entry process and faster acquisition of competitive advantage.

We operate in an expanding and demanding environment that requires fast responsive actions to develop and maintain competitive advantage in the international market place. The advantage of new companies to allocate and identify resources and implementation plans suitable in a range of environments simultaneously is a critical component of success.

There may be times when size and experience will play a major role in market penetration within specific sectors but generally youth and flexibility are an advantage especially within the realm of technology based service industries.

As Zahara (2003) concluded that Oviatt & McDougall (1994) have started an important and influential research stream, whose contributions have been insightful, powerful and varied." It should be recognized that while these observations are an important part of assessing INV's we must keep evaluating and developing mechanisms of market entry to challenge existing market leaders.

In conclusion we can assume that the findings and theories of Oviatt & McDougall (1993) and supported by Zahra (2005) are a valid assessment of the requirements for INV's.

Foreign direct investment and the multinational enterprise

Investment Benefit

Engagement in FDI for corporations is driven by the seeking of competitive advantage, and, for recipient countries the motivation can be seen as social and local economic gain, especially within the developing economies.

In a global economy FDI plays a significant role in furthering the concept of globalization and to a certain extent the social enhancement of the recipient country. however, the political ramifications of this process can have an adverse effect on both the investor and host country. While these factors play a role in deciding the nature of FDI for corporations the overwhelming factor will be the identification of potential competitive advantage.

Whether the FDI is horizontal or vertical there are going to be issues that will need to be addressed in relation to PR and the perceived impact at home and at the host country. The closure of plants in one country and transfer to another will have varying negative impacts for the organisation and government in one country and an opposite positive potential in the new country.

The drive by host countries to develop FDI potential has resulted in the creation of Bilateral Investment Treaties (BIT's). These treaties are designed to balance the rights of foreign investor with the host countries domestic investors. While these treaties may go some way in assuring potential investors there appears to be only a slim connection between BIT's and FDI as concluded by Tobin & Rose-Ackerman (2003) "BIT's appear to be important instruments for riskier countries that wish to attract FDI, but, in general, they may not fulfill their major objective" Although BIT's may not show a significant increase in FDI it does show that firms need to be secure in their investment and that the stability and legal structure of the host country is going to impact on the decision to invest.

With the need to grow and develop markets the advantages for firms to expand into new geographic areas for the achievement of greater market targets and production advantage is a reality of globalization We have seen major car manufactures moving and developing manufacturing plants on a global scale to obtain competitive advantage in differing target markets.

FDI seems to offer positive advantages for firms providing there is security of investment, As de Mello Jr (1999) identifies that providing the following factors are accounted for, Political risk, policy structure, trade regime and institutional structure , then FDI can offer advantages for firms. FDI plays a role in the economic development of a host country concluded by Carkovik and Levine (n.d) "there is a positive link between FDI and growth." FDI is a necessary part of globalization, no matter what advantages and benefits host countries receive the driving influence will be the security and return for investing corporations in terms of profit and competitive advantage.

Environments of international business

Asset stripping or sustainable growth? - The FDI question.

Issues around the benefits of governments generating employment through subsidy incentives to foreign corporations and investors is a contentious matter in many quarters. The returns to the economic output of the country should show that the return on the subsidy outweighs the initial subsidy, however, governments do not necessarily offer and operate on the basis of financial return. Social and political advantage will go a long way to justify government expenditure. When issues of unemployment are concerned the motivation for governments to be seen as "doing something" means that political payback may play a major role in inward investment strategy. With the closure of coal mines in Wales during the eighties the drive for inward investment and job creation played a significant part in regenerating areas affected by the mine closure. This regeneration involved a move to service industries like call centre operations and technology based assembly units, this provided relieve to a population that was facing high unemployment but did nothing to establish a long-term sustainable economy. When the going got tough and subsidies reduce the corporations left. FDI is an exploitative program that asset strips the local communities.

Haskel et al (2007) assessment using ARD and ONS data may reflect more biased and incomplete data because of the governments needs to justify its FDI strategy. While ARD and ONS are independent there will always be questions on data supportive of government policy. Although the balances and awareness of bias have been accounted for at various stages of investigation one should be aware that bias adjustment may well create bias. Statistical assessment of bigger economic issues that are driven by political will and social development may not reflect true economic advantage to FDI on the host nation while the true winner is the corporation receiving the subsidy and market advantages from attracting government departments.

Applying FDI as a means of gaining political advantage has been questioned by Phelps & Tewdwr- Jones (2001)"It is noteworthy just how much prestige has been and continues to be placed on inward investments by RDAs and the government as flagship economic development projects when compared to support for indigenous firms." How government promote FDI to there public seems to ignore the true economic situation as pointed out by Haskel et al (2007) "the per-job value of spillovers are less than per-job incentives governments have granted in recent high-profile cases." This could be seen as evident with the government encouragement of foreign car manufacturers to replace the demised home spun car manufacturing industry.

Inward investment has been used as a tool to alleviate social unrest and dissatisfaction of government economic policy is a concern that to a certain degree is addressed by Haskel et al (2007) while collecting data "The first and most important is to reiterate that these calculations are only suggestive, as they rely on many assumptions and caveats." The assumptions around returns from subsidy input show that even with the limited information FDI is not profitable for governments who instigate subsidy. For FDI to achieve benefit for its host it must be operationally sustainable without the creation of an artificial reality through the "propping up" strategy of promoting FDI through uncompetitive government support. The research and its underlying nature confirms my view that within the UK FDI was a politically motivated act that did not show any advantageous elements to the long-term economic stability of the nation.

Environments of international business

Cultural Environment

Inward investment within a country can face cultural barriers in the initial stages of development. There will always be social questions around the motivation of the MNE's that settle in areas of social deprivation. Questions by some of the community around motivations of foreign companies and possible different ways of dealing with management - worker relations.

During the eighties in Wales there was a massive reduction and closure of the mining industry and a highly unprofitable state owned steel industry. The result was a high level of unemployment and social unrest. There was a policy of attracting FDI to replace the lost industries, however, the available workforce was mainly manual and the trend was to create low skill employment environments Huggins (2001) "only 14% of newly located plants had a workforce already in

place that was sufficiently highly skilled for the plants' particular needs", that resulted in up skilling opportunities and vocational training programmes. From a cultural and historical point there was a collective awareness of previous foreign exploitation from the English industrialist. Any investor would be wise to accommodate the fears and concerns of the community. In fact with larger Japanese, Korean and other Asian countries, investing heavily in assembly factories, managed to reduce these fears and establish good management - worker practices not possible with the previous structures around unionization Education plays a significant role in establishing a MNE in a new host country in relation to the communities perception.

Investing in an area that has suffered exploitation require careful and sensitive management. By offering educational packages and encouraging up-skilling and skill shifting opportunities companies and communities bonded. Huggins (2001) "It was found that the large majority of foreign-owned plants in Wales (88%) have utilized aftercare training and skills development initiatives"

There is also a tendency towards a lack of local commercial development that means there are opportunities for MNE's to develop new operations in relatively competitive free environment. Calkins & Wiener (1998) "Welsh agencies agree that cultural as well as structural values have impeded the development of indigenous industry."

Korean company LG became a major investor in Wales in 1996 by promising to create 6100 jobs for an investment of £1.7billion. Although the was a skill mismatch in the area, education mechanisms where embedded into the community to assist the companies development. Phelps et al (1998) identify that as a result of this FDI A semiconductor training centre was established and local universities provided industry specific degrees. All of this was a result of significant government grants and subsidies made to LG and training agencies.

Short comings in social and cultural environments should not be a barrier to investment. Where there is a skill shortage training and corporate development can play a major part in establishing and integrating new MNE's into Wales as seen by the LG example . Unfortunately this is not always the case and it has resulted in the lack of spillover advantage and entrepreneurial development. By educating and encouraging the workforce the MNE will establish a more sustainable and innovative presence within the country.

Stable strategy with a third leg.

When an organisation enters a new foreign market it is faced with many structural and strategic issues. Traditionally companies faced resource and market penetration issues for successful activity, however, one area that was regarded as a secondary issue was that of the institutional bodies that directly and indirectly accommodate the commercial functionality of the state and industry. There needs to be a greater understanding of the local legal, political and social environment for MNE's to sustainably enter new foreign areas of operation.

As Peng et al (2008) point out "Institutions are much more than background conditions" They go on to say that institutions directly influence the strategy of an organisation to help create competitive advantage. This competitive advantage is only achievable in a sustainable way when strategies placate local institutions and communities. This could be seen as being more crucial in emerging and developing economies where free market approaches are new and not fully understood. The concept of creating a tripod strategy that takes into account Competition, Resources and Institutions seems a sound system for succeeding in the effective establishment of a new organisational presence within a new market.

(1) Antidumping as entry barriers;

Peng et al (2008) examines four areas that take into account the need to accommodate the assessment and inclusion of institutional mechanisms within any developed strategy. Each area explores the mechanisms of controlling MNE's into participating within the cultural, social and economic environments of the host.

Anti dumping legislation can be used as a method of protectionism by the host country, while there may be cases of attempted market manipulation by market entrees, the exploitation of the law can be prohibitive of free trade. It is imperative for the MNE to fully understand the impact of there market entry on local companies and their relationship and communication mechanisms with local and national institutions. Peng et al (2008) quoting (Schuler et al., (2002) were right to assume that "when industry- and resource-based weapons fail, there is a direct implication for domestic firms under competitive pressures from imports: An institution-based view of international business strategy launch an institution-based missile by filing an antidumping petition ".The use of an institution as a means of reaching or maintaining competitive advantage is a counter productive strategy that can have greater negative impact on future trading partnerships.

(2) Competing in and out of India;

If we look at India then we see the negative issues of success. When institutions successfully implement strategies that enable local companies use local resources to develop products and services that become global powerhouses then external institutions will embark on limiting or even prohibiting market entry for that nation and establish restrictions in outbound FDI. Understanding that institutions are fluid and mechanisms of control and policies are not always consistent or permanent. While openness increases growth opportunity it can be exploited when success needs to be controlled.

(3) Growing the firm in China;

When institution mechanisms are poor then there opportunities for interpersonal networking structures to informally establish protocols can be seen in China, this maybe a cultural development but may well evolve into more formal institutional organisations that will impact on future trade development. In fact Peng et al (2008) recognise that market entrants will need to establish links with the informal inter-organisational bodies "as evidenced by the numerous international strategic alliances with local firms" Understanding and communicating with local structures is paramount to successful market entry, however, as local markets and organisation evolve it is vital that MNE's keep the fingers on the pulse of local political and legal activity.

(4) Governing the corporation in emerging economies.

Corporate governance may well operate effectively within modern trading organisations comfortable with, and adapted to, dispersed ownership. However, New and emerging economies may find the concept difficult and alien. The concept of singular or minority control of an organisation that shows little or no transparency will tend to be the norm in emerging markets. The difficulty will arise primarily arise between principles of the organisation. I tend to agree with Peng et al (2008) who cite Morck et al.,(2005); Young et al., (2008) that "In emerging economies, governance reforms need to find ways to reduce (certainly not increase!) such concentrated shareholding in the hands of controlling shareholders" Failure to enact a more transparent and open policy on governance will on hinder emerging organisations and host nations.

Peng et al (2008) highlight the importance in assimilating the policies, laws and social treats of local venues for MNE's. It becomes imperative the there is an harmonious relationship between corporations and institutions. This relationship will promote understanding and enhance the development and enactment of strategies within the operating market.

In relation to governmental or local interference to protect local interests one can assume that this will yield short term political advantage, but eventually leads to reduced economic activity that inhibits globalization and free trade. It is almost a requirement for MNE's to take on board the issues as seen by local and national institutions.

Global integration and international finance

Financial Crisis

Financial mechanisms employed on the global markets are the communicators of institutional and organisational policies and strategies. The current situation is a reflection of poor political and managerial understanding or corrupt self motivated and miss managed regulation of commercial financial institutions around the world. While many see the origins of the the current crisis as being manifested because of the sub prime lending policies, especially within the banking institutions of the United States. These actions where carried out through greed motivation of banking staff and poor and ineffective control systems by regulatory bodies and governments. As Reinhart & Roghoff (2008) point out factors behind the crisis "It also follows a well-trodden path laid down by centuries of financial folly."

The result of this miss management as resulted in the slowing of national economies and a majority of businesses on a global scale, resulting in increases in unemployment, reduced borrowing opportunities for emerging and developing organisations. The social implications will reflect on government policy which may not result in the most sensible long-term solutions. The political desire to be seen to do something with a short term positive result will only help increase votes for the ruling party and may not result in a stable and sustainable economy. We have seen the scenario of boom and bust many times and all of this is predominantly driven for short term political gain.

The concept of free trade becomes challenged when home countries see the activities of other nations being able to produce products more efficiently because this effects in a negative manner the output of domestic product. This will result in the political institutions introducing trade restricting and blocking rules to help domestic organisations, with the result that retaliatory actions are then instigated, resulting a more downward and restricted global economy. Although during the current crisis there has been a verbal resistance to trade restrictions in the traditional sense, nations are moving back to the concept of 'Buy products produced here'. This could be seen has a form of restrictive manipulation to trade.

When faced with financial crisis the stabilization of markets becomes the paramount concern of controlling institutions. In this particular case the need to heavily support and in some cases nationalize and underwrite banks has in itself created some uncertainty. This uncertainty will require the application of new, more responsible and stronger regulatory mechanisms on local, national and international levels. As Taylor (2008) concludes "Most urgently it is important to

reinstate or establish a set of principles to follow to prevent misguided actions and interventions

in the future" .It could be argued that if you remove the commercial profit term from the banking sector and replace it with a developmental motivation under control of national governments it would help reduces the future risks of damage to economies. An alternative would be to establish banks along the lines of the Credit Union movement and remove the profit motivation and high incentives.

The current crisis highlights the short comings of the current global financial institutions. To enable a truly global economy that fully exploits free trade there will need to be a radical rethink of how these institutions act and relate to governments. Free trade can only be damaged by the global financial sensitivity that has been demonstrated by both the Asian and Global crises. The emerging economies will become more economically interrelated with established markets and more vulnerable to the historical financial and economic cycles. This was highlighted by Fidrmuc & Korhonen (2009) "the global economy may be moving to a situation characterized by increasing interdependencies between developed and emerging economies." To be in a position of global financial stability we must overhaul and adapt our trading and regulatory systems.

Contagion Crisis

The concept of financial contagion as an explanation of reactions and situational fiscal positioning is explored in relation to the Mexican, Asian and Russian crises. The assumption that financial linkages to a country undergoing financial crisis contribute to higher probability of cross border crisis expansion is explored. It seems a logical assumption that the knock on effects of a crisis will manifest in commercially and economically related organisations and institutions. This symbiotic bonding of currencies and financial relationships play a significant role in the regional interpretation and implementation of future fiscal strategies at all levels of trade. The understanding of the fundamental causes of crisis transmission will allow for more effective management and prevention of future negative financial events.

Investors looking on a regional basis need to make judgements on the cause and effect scenarios related to a particular situation to fully benefit from crisis situations. While the argument from Caramazza et al (2004) that "The common creditor is the most important and significant variable" it is not going to be the only factor to accommodate in investor reactionary strategy to a financial crisis. While the general concept would be a process of damage limitation on the part of the investor which may involve withdrawal thus impacting, potentially, on deepening the crisis. as a result of knee jerk reactions from investors as Caramazza et al (2004) point out "some countries, therefore, may experience capital outflows"

The assessment of empirical evidence by Caramazza et al (2004) focusing on the Identifying Crisis, Measuring the common creditor and their importance along with the Implied probability of crisis and Robustness goes towards understanding the inter relationships of financial processes and reactions. The implication that no one factor is instrumental to crisis transmission we must understand that perceptions to crisis as well as factual interpretation will factor into investor reactions.

The assumption that common creditor is key to financial contagion is based on current commercial interpretation mechanisms. Building on the understanding of the interpretation systems and their effects on cross border transmission will allow us to rethink and modify the standard response mechanisms employed by investors today and allow for the development of more sustainable and stable financial and currency transactions. Thus, helping stabilize economic environments.

The methods employed by Caramazza et al (2004) face the situation in a way that removes the original country. This may allow for knock on assessment but by not allowing for additional internal cause factors e.g political and perceptive positions, the true picture may not be fully visible. To fully understand contagion we must look deeper and wider for a true and consolidated position on the intricacies of international cross border financial evolution.

Concluding that situations in one financial environment will impact on surrounding financial environments is a fair and correct assumption, however, we must not view situations in a segmented and independent manner. Like most things in live the bigger picture can give better clues to the reactionary situations, it is the detail that we can be lost in and miss the whole picture and the most effective reactions. Caramazza et al (2004) conclusions may well be valid in their terms of reference but not in relation to the bigger picture of the three crises they were evaluating.

The concept of contagion is assessed in different ways and there fore the concept needs to be standardized for a fuller academic and comparative assessment. Kaminsky & Reinhart (1998) "contagion has been understood to be different things across different studies" Transmission of financial disease is not to be viewed in isolation there are many factors that may well increase and decrease it 's progress, including social and political environments.

International business strategies

Strategy Operations

Starbucks have successfully and rapidly entered the international arena with a tactically aggressive expansion programme. The venturing into and sustaining a global operation requires flexibility and innovation. The process of developing and sustaining strategies that are, or potentially, diverse requires a significant amount of organisational cultural tolerance and understanding. identifying an appropriate national strategy that compliments the fundamentals of the parent company is a key strategical process. Deciding on the method of entering and timing of entry into a particular market will be the key drivers in whether the organisation gains competitive advantage. Maximizing on market place opportunities and identifying key players and potential partners would be a major element when reviewing potential markets.

When markets become saturated organisations need to look for new operating environments. Gupta and Govindarajan (2000)"Today, globalization is no longer an option but a strategic imperative for all but the smallest firms" There are many criteria involved in developing a new customer sectors and globalization offers opportunities to many companies. Even for organisations trading in many countries the development of new country markets may well offer new tactical and cultural issues. Over coming this issues will form the basis of the 'introduction strategy' development. One approach would be in the identification of modes of entry that benefit from local experience. By developing relationships with local players the company can gain significant advantage. The fundamentals of entry can be identified as Location, timing and mode of market entry. The successful analysis of these factors could well determine the level of commercial success.

The successful identification of a partner for entry is going to be one of the key steps, next it is to look at the structure of that partnership. Deciding on partnerships, licensing or franchising will depend among other things on the commitment of both parties and the cultural environment being entered. The Starbucks entry strategy is identified by Dutta and Subhadra (N.D) "Starbucks decided to enter international markets by using a three pronged strategy:Joint Ventures, Licensing and wholly owned subsidies" There are many risks associated with international markets such as

Operational, Political, country, technological and Environmental (Dutta and Subhadra (N.D)). By using native partnerships allows for greater understanding of the cultural trends and reactions to influencing situations. However, by diluting the shareholding the is a risk that profits will not be a complete as if a wholly owned operations was active. Dutta and Subhadra (N.D)"Analysts observed that Starbucks was unable to earn enough revenues from its international operations due to complex joint ventures and licensing agreements."

While the success of Starbucks is apparent on many street corners its future strategy in terms of international expansion will need to be reviewed. The current mechanisms work in terms of market entry but may not be sustainable through the Joint Venture or Licensing track unless there is a reworking of the agreements. The brand strength should now empower them to negotiate more favorable terms. However, it must be recognized that successful entry for Starbucks does not mean that it will be a sustainable position. They must look to regaining ownership where possible. Barkema et al (1997)"International wholly owned subsidiaries allow firms to learn how to operate in foreign settings without the complexities of cooperating with a partner"

Global financial management and accounting

Payment Methods

The issues around trade payment security is a critical factor for MNE's. Where price margins are low there becomes increased sensitivity to currency fluctuations and guarantee payment methods. Globalization and technological advances allow for a potential seamless transfer of funds. Giovannucci (n.d) "As new technologies and advances in communications are changing trade logistics and speeding and facilitating transactions, businesses are finding new opportunities and new ways to operate." However, distance and detached commercial activity requires that both parties in a transaction feel secure and confident in the designated transaction process. These process' are instrumental in maintaining efficient and profitable trading.

The resources available to assist in secure international trade payments are focused on 5 key areas as highlighted by Giovannucci (n.d) Cash in advance, Letter of credit, Documentary collection, Open account or credit, Counter trade or Barter. There becomes a practical and strategic process in defining which mechanism is most beneficial to the organisation. Issues also around invoicing strategy also come into play, the choice of currency will play a part in ensuring a solidified value to the product being traded in terms of value assessment . Exposure to risk should be minimized by all parties although the necessities of global trade and pricing strategies may require payment options that are potentially risky for one party. This may well impact on the strategical continuance issues regarding forward pricing models for the purchaser. Accounting for potential losses due to non fulfillment of contractual obligations will be a critical part of managing the process.

Deciding on the mechanism for payment is going to impact on pricing, in particular, relating to how and in what form/ currency is used, along ,with credit financing of larger projects. The financing through the banking system or government guarantee systems can assist MNE's to enter markets that would normally offer high risk environments. The use of such systems will as been a widely used mechanism for MNE's expansion strategies. Organizations should strategically measure the impact and consequentness of its invoicing and payment strategies to meet is production, financial and fulfillment targets. Invoicing in a specific non home currency may offer some solidity to transactions when several customers over a range of countries as highlighted by Grosse and Behrman (1992)"exchange risk assessment acquires a new dimension when operations are spread over several types of INC (International contractor) activities or in several different countries."

While there are a plethora of payment and financing options for organisations the driving factor is going to be protecting the organisation both as a purchaser and provider. Identifying the suitable vehicle for an organisations international payment and invoicing methods must play a major role in its international trading strategies. Although Hauner (2002) points out "For trade in manufactured goods between MDCs, the major part of contracts are denominated in the exporter's currency and most of the remaining contracts are denominated in the importer's currency, while third-currency invoicing is relatively rare ("Grassman's Law").I would suggest that third country currency may offer a more secure and beneficial mechanism for MNE's.

Global marketing, supply chain, and human resources

Global Marketing

The issues for an MNE's marketing operations can vary depending on the product and the environment it is released into. It becomes critical to asses the brand in terms of language and cultural values. These issues are more problematic with the movement of established brands from one country to another. Many marketing complications can be more readily addressed with new internationally focused products. The transference of products into a new market should need to fit with the strategy employed in the original market, if changes are needed to incorporate the product then an organisations marketing strategy should be locally based and focus on the cultural and social interpretation of the brand. Palich & Gomez-Mejia (1999) "one of the most important challenges organizations face is that of effectively managing cultural diversity."

Understanding the target market within a local context means that the introduction of established brands should migrate smoothly if conditions of culture and language are addressed. With globalization comes a desire from a marketing perspective to establish an almost generic process through brand standardization As Jain (1989) points out "the decision on standardization should be based on economic pay off, which includes financial performance, competitive advantage, and other aspects." We can see many products and brand with an almost universal image around the globe, however, it must recognized that this form of marketing many well work, the ability to manipulate and modify strategies to a local audience may offer better product placement and competitive advantage. Rather than going down the route of 'genetically' modifying brands to fit a global view marketeers should be adapting strategies to the environment and engendering local values and perceptions instead of global stereo typing.

The successful implementation of an international marketing strategy should recognise the cultural fluidity and diversity of the country or region the organisation is entering. Campaigns that try to establish alien concepts and values will under achieve in the short term. The embedding of a new brand that has a well established international reputation may prove easier to introduce, but for strong establishment it will still require 'localizing'

The addition of many more variables in to an international marking environment means that the marketing manager must understand a growing number of cultural, political and social conditions. While understanding the diversity of environments it also becomes important to reduce the number of conflicting points in a product introduction thus smoothing the transition from one market to another. This is highlighted by Schuiling & Kapferer (2004) "there are many reasons to encourage the development of brand portfolios that contain a balanced mix of strong local and international brands." By engaging a mix of messages it becomes easier to convey a value for a product that meets a greater audience and reduces the risk of customer isolation.

Emerging issues and risks

E Commerce

The birth of e-commerce and internet trading could be described as the time of mass entrepreneurial rising. The empowerment of individuals and SME's in a globalized economy offers challenges to MNE's. The flexibility of smaller organisations over more cumbersome international bodies means that competitive advantage of MNE's can be more vulnerable to challenges via the internet. This new tool of communication and international trading platform offers enormous potential to all who can master its environment. In the early days of the commercialization of the web it was the forward thinking entrepreneurial organisations that became leaders in the media and it was left to the established MNE's to go through a period of catch up.

The dream of e-commerce has not been a smooth path and in fact it raise many issues for the supplier and consumer. For the supplier issues around global image and product conformity begin to play a growing part in the international marketing strategy of the organisation as raised by Lo & Kao (2008) "any e-businesses operating on the Internet have a growing international presence and cannot ignore their global marketing image." The consumer faces issues of trust and security along with assessing the credibility of the supplier. Teo &Liu (2007) "The concept of trust is crucial because it affects a number of factors essential to online transactions, including security and privacy."

Dealing with the above issues is only part of the picture faced by users of e-commerce, for effective and economic application it becomes important for the establishment of functioning and stable infrastructure. This as been recognized by many governments who are embarking on programmes to ensure that a high percentage of their population have access to fast stable internet connections. This has been a strategy employed by emerging economies such as China. Ng (2009) "A positive trend of e-commerce can assist the sustainability of growth in the country's international trade."

Today the need for an NME to have a web strategy is as vital as any other part of it organisational structure. As for the SME the NME face similar factors when entering the e-commerce field. Wilson et al (2008) "Where technology-related factors are significant, they tend to relate to skills availability rather than finance or availability of appropriate software." Over coming the technological issues and being able to resource the online presence and its required logistical support structures then offers an effective channel of sales and promotion activities for an organisations international trading.

The web has become the face or shop window of most organisations and providing there is continuing support of governments in the development and building of the infrastructure, much like the development and building of interstate highways in the USA, there will be fast economic payback.

Has we as individuals become more comfortable with online trading and feel secure in the transactions then e-commerce will continue to play a major part in the sales and product promotion of the majority of international traders.

We have seen rapid growth of e-commerce offer the last seven years and all indicators are that it will continue to grow. The way in which organisation approach their entry into this sector will have a lasting influence on their success. This is not an area that easily translates the conventional marketing approaches and requires new and customized approaches that meet and address the fears of the customer, who now has more power, influence and choice.

Chapter 4

Economic Management

Firm Theory

Organisational sustainability and growth are paramount in the modern firm. How this is achieved is a critical function of the organisations management. Mechanisms for delivering such goals are based on the functional experience and theoretical knowledge of the management team. Understanding the dynamics of organisational activities and interaction at both an internal and external level will assist in achieving competitive advantage. Deciding on short term maximized profits to facilitate corporate value for shareholders or playing the "long game" of developing and strengthening the long-term survival and profitability of the organisation is a balancing act that does not exclusively fall into either camp. Balancing short-term value generation with long-term sustainability is achieved by the manager by drawing on sound theoretical knowledge and innovative action implementation.

Looking at the theories of the firm as a method or tool to achieving objectives of the organisation is a critical element of management processes. If the prime driver of management is to add value for shareholders then we can apply processes that allow the attaining of such goals within the resources and activities of the organisation. The question that springs to mind is, Is it in the best interests of the shareholders to risk sustainability for short-term maximized profits? How we use these theory's is based on our managerial experience As Grant (1996) points out "Economic theories of the firm are concerned primarily with predicting the behavior of firms in external markets. " If we wish to predict firms interaction with its external audience then how we apply and experience these theoretical assumptions can dictate the philosophical and strategic planning of the organisation.

One of the key theory influencers has been the neoclassical theory, however we should also look towards other theories that accommodate the rapidly changing global environment. Evolutionary economic theory can play a critical role is assisting the development and strategic planing of the organisation. Nelson (2008) introduces us the the concept "Sanjaya Lall believed that economic development had to be understood as an evolutionary process, with technological learning at its core, and that standard neoclassical economics was completely inadequate as a theory of the key processes and institutions involved"

Introducing polices based on theoretical assumptions can be restricting to any organisation. While they can guide a manage and help asses and predict to a certain degree behavioral functions and value developmental mechanisms they cannot replace the experience and market understanding of experienced managers.

Operating on the concept of short-term value enhancement for the short-term benefit of shareholders is a an attractive proposition for the performance driven organisation it can pose potential risks for the longevity of the firm.

There must be a balance between short-term value maximization and long-term sustainability. Both are symbiotic activities that contribute to the healthy actions and results of the modern organisation. Failure to account for inputs that facilitate both drivers will fundamentally weaken the organisation. In fact the learning from experience and creative innovation should contribute to the strategy of successful participation in the market as highlighted by Foss & Klein (2004) "the economic theory of the firm can be improved substantially by taking seriously the essential heterogeneity of capital goods and the subsequent need for entrepreneurial experimentation" Therefore, there is no defining classification of superiority only compatibility through harmonized interaction.

Optimization Analysis

The over all objective for an organisation is to operate efficiently and cost effectively, whether that is in generation of profit or through delivery objectives. Being able the optimize the activity parameters will guide the organisation to a level of harmonious functionality. Part of the process used to analyze the current activity and future output potential will be to asses the factors around the concept of total, average and marginal values. Using this data we can work towards the level of optimized functionality.

By analyzing the different elements between total, average and marginal costs and their relationship to attaining optimized functionality we can break down and reconstruct production and sales mechanisms that offer better profitability or service efficiency. As we measure the total cost and derive the average cost per item by dividing the total cost (TC) by the number of items produced we obtain the average cost (AC) We calculate the marginal cost (MC) by dividing the change in TC by the change in the number of items.

Being able to understand and predict the scale and effect of increasing production and how the increase can impact on profitability is a critical part of organisational development planning and strategic market activities. Using the total, average and marginal cost as a guide to efficiency assessment and part of the optimization process is a fundamental in the economic planning and predicting of the organisation. Using the total, average and marginal concepts as a means of optimizing production in terms of economies of scale is an effective way to achieve competitive advantage in terms of production costs and retail pricing. The benefits of marginal costing was highlighted by Panzar and Willig (1977) when assessing multi scale outputs "successfully characterizes the profitability of marginal cost pricing"

Understanding and identifying the limits of the organisation through being able to optimize activity through quantifiable methods is a useful tool in the tool kit of of the modern global manager. Many factors come into play in the over all strategy of the organisation, but a sound base of identified known factors allows for the development of more creative and innovative operating solutions.

Once we are aware of the fundamentals of our organisations production dynamics we can better plan and predict the future needs and resource requirements of the organisation. The use of the concepts discussed here and their incorporation into analyzing operations for the optimization of the activities of the firm is a practical way of defining a sound base for achieving competitive advantage.

Demand Theory

The process of estimating and identifying demand is an instrumental part of the managers activity when devising future sales and marketing strategy. By calculating future demand accurately organisations will maximise efficiency within all the delivery mechanisms. Because the variables associated with market movement and consumer selectivity it becomes more complex than straight forward on ward projection assessment. When we see variations in both supply and demand, predictions need to be made with additional information and theories from other related sources. Being unable to identify problems associated with calculating a demand curve may result in under or over stating of demand. Such variables as demographics as introduced by Pollak and Wales (1981) "demographic variables such as family size and age composition are major determinants of household consumption patterns." Variations in demand can be influenced by other factors than price, however, we can see the correlation between price reduction and demand increasing a general market situation.

On the bases that any change in price will influence the demand for a product we can calculate the resulting demand changes through a demand curve. However, the simple act of changing price in a sophisticated market is not going to give a standardized answer in relation to demand. Factors that influence demand, such as demographics, competition quality and the elasticity of price changes within the target market. The critical part of identifying the elements that impact on these calculations can become problematic. Also, the application of information that is unquantifiable will result in poor, inaccurate results as concluded by Epple (1987) "If important characteristics are unmeasured and they are correlated with measured characteristics, the coefficients on measured characteristics will be biased. "

As demand for a product can vary in a time frame, with peaks and troughs over a given period the demand curve will only give an over view of the total demand of the product which does not take into account the seasonal or promotional related events. The resulting identification problem should be addressed by allowing for shifts or differ in a unrestricted manner as highlighted by Salvadore (2007)

Understanding the requirements needed to asses the demand of a product in relation to time and other environmental influences traditionally requires the application of regression analysis as a mode of attaining corrected information. As Freedman (2004) says most people know "that causal mechanisms can be inferred from non-experimental data by running regressions." Although he goes on to question the traditional application of regression calculations, however, we can see that the traditional assumptions of influencing factors can be included and accounted for and play a major role in predicting future demand.

When calculating demand the inference or even bias arising from identification problems can lead to inaccurate assumptions which will "knock on" in the strategy and logistics of the firm. Not having product available on time or even hold too much product when demand is low. Many influences impact on demand and issues around identification problems and other environmental issues can be factored into calculations, but we should remember the use of the demand curve is a tool and not an oracle for the manager.

Diminishing Returns

Organizations strife to maximise returns for its stakeholders. The act of production, whether goods or services, should operate at the most efficient level possible to fully utilize resources and maximise profit. It is well recognized that there comes a point in production where the inputs are producing less efficient returns for the firm. This patten was recognized as far back as 1776 and the laws of diminishing returns was proposed by Turgot as identified by Shephard and Fare (1974). The impact of diminishing returns on the production strategy means that efficient use of resources helps place the firm in a strong competitive environment. Once we apply the law of diminishing returns, that is accept that there will be a point at which over all output value will begin to decrease against inputs that are not variable or are fixed within the term of production, we can establish production to ensure that output is optimized in relation to achieving a profitable scenario.

The acknowledgement that increasing investment will lead to a reduction in the value of output is a classical approach of economics in management. For the manager to apply the law of diminishing returns to the firms production programme and within the framework of production theory it is necessary to establish the parameters of the production process. While identifying the variable inputs of the production process and establishing the fixed inputs, these fixed input may be fixed only for the term of the production run. In a simplistic way the output is derived from the input of labour and capital as described by Salvatore (2007). Of course this is a basic description that would apply to all production functions with varying degrees of sophistication and complication, however, it has been suggested that the application of the law of diminishing return is less applicable in larger stronger organisations, This assumption is that larger corporations are more capable of maintaining the variable inputs in such a way as they become fixed within the life cycle of the product. This may be the case but the impact of of the law will still apply in that there becomes a optimized point of production, the calculation is easier, but the outcome is the same, at some point the continued production results in less return on production investment.

The analyzing of groups of variants within the production process is going to be fundamental to the goal of optimized production. Fundamentally the relationship between labour and capital inputs are key to the optimized output, actions to reduce labour will impact on output in a conventional sense, however enhanced output can be achieved by introducing automated systems that are less reliable on manual labour, hence reducing the element of variable labour costs and increasing the fixed capital costs. All of these elements allow the organisation to enact actions towards optimized production and maximized profits.

The relationship between diminishing return and production is tied in the need to achieve the most efficient and profitable production run possible for the organisation. The implications of the relationship is the optimized production process. This allows for the assigning of the most efficient price setting to help enhance competitive advantage.

Short Run

While perfect environments are not a reality in the business world the ability to compare the theory of a situation that reflects a perfect state allows us to strife for perfection within the working environments. Reaching an optimized price within a short run scenario for an organisation that is either close to being in a perfect competition scenario or when operating in a monopolistic market situation is a paramount element of achieving the goal of optimized operating function. Although each operating area offer different market activity processes being able to optimize a short run price that fits the market of activity is a fundamental to market acceptance.

To understand the implications of the short run price determinant we must isolate the market activity and competition areas. The different operating scenarios between a theoretical perfect competition firm and one that operates in a monopolistic way need to be identified and applied to the calculation of price sustainability and viability for the firms customers.

Understanding the short run price determining factors associated with the construction methods used to ascertain a price is achieved with specific criteria linked to each area of the firms production environments.

Although the perfect competition firm is a theoretical construction there are firms that can and do operate in a 'nearly perfect competition' environment. This is a market where no single participant can determine a price control and where entry and exit methods to the market of relatively easy and where there is a large body of sellers and buyers. As Salvadore (2007) the closest we can get to a perfect competition scenario is with the stock market, but as he points out there are factors that move the market away from the definition. To attribute a price within a close to position requires that there is an understanding that selling above or below the short run price will result in either a reduction in sales demand or reduction in profit efficiently. The establishment of a price in a short run context within the perfection competition market is paramount as long term economic profit is not possible.

The realistic approach of a company operating in an exclusive monopolistic market does so with a relative comfort factor in terms of its customer acceptance of the prices set by the monopoly. Although setting prices on predictive short run programmes such as wholesale electricity prices in state owned generating companies is an example where setting the price on variable production costs i.e changes in oil, gas or coal. The firm may control the delivery of generated power but must also account for legislation that moderates the retail pricing guidelines. In this market where different distributors purchase from the generator it is critical to know the amount of power required and thus price the available power. García-Martos et al (2007) establish that "A generating company can better decide its bidding price when having accurate one-day-ahead forecasts. This ability to set a price suitable to the variabilities of the market costs means that the consumer is able to have prices that reflect the cost variables in a more real-time event horizon. Although García-Martos et al (2007) identify two models to determine prices associated with demand on weekdays and weekends "We recommend computing forecasts for working days with model 48 (using only weekdays) and with model 24 for weekends (using complete weeks).

Applying the following determines the establishment of short run price in each of the market sectors we have explored

Perfect Competition

The determination of price is based on the intersection of market demand curve and the market supply curve. Once the equilibrium price is set there is no incentive for a firm to vary the price. This is defined in Salvadore (2007) as the firm being a 'Price taker'

Monopolistic Market.

Within the monopoly area a price is set not as a 'price taker' but can set its price to maximise profits in the short run and account for any long term situations. The relationship to establish price in this case is determined by the market demand curve and the marginal revenue curve. Price is established at a point halfway between MR and MD curve. This would enable maximization of profits.

We can see the need to establish in differing ways the short run price in each of the situations we have explored. Only by understanding the implications of the price set for the market can we work towards optimized delivery mechanisms.

Cartel Cheating

Cartels take a very controversial position in the commercial world. Seen as either a mechanism for maintaining control and unnatural profits within a sector or as a way of protecting volatile markets for the interests of all. Of course the corporate culture to generate profit can play a dual role in the operation of the cartel, it can ensure that all members share in the market place or where there is an identified weakness in the market member over riding drive for profit may encourage them to employ mechanisms that exploit a weakness in the cartel or member organisation for its own increased market share or profit.

The protectionist policy of the cartel is there to ensure control, both or either commercial and political, in a potentially manipulative or vulnerable market. Whether the style of cartel is centralized or market-sharing the desire to protect is strong in a perfect operating environment. Although the concept of the cartel is seen differently and even illegal in some states, it does exist and operate as some of the most influential global bodies. With so much power the need for internal control is critical. When the market is operating within the expected or predicted values and members of the cartel are healthy then the need to operate outside of the cartels rules is reduced, once there is a breakdown in operating health or there is political or commercial instability there is opportunity for individual members to carry out individual actions that are not in the group interest of the cartel . This could be seen as cheating and putting the power of the cartel at jeopardy. The cartels ability to fix price and or supply of a product and limit the entrants to market is only truly beneficial to its members, its customers are exposed to inflated prices and controlled supply, however, if this is removed and a free trade environment is established each firm that was part of the cartel becomes exposed to issues of supply, price and demand. This can influence the level of profit and leaves the firm in a much more exposed position that is free from protective mechanisms.

Advantages of cartel establishment may have significant advantages for the cartel members when organisations come together in R&D, rather than controlling market the cartel can control the technological output within the market as Kamien et al (1992) states "Analysis of pure-strategy sub game-perfect Nash equilibria discloses that for sufficiently high spillover rates the reduction in unit costs is greater under R&D cartelization than under R&D competition." This can be seen as a benefit for the consumer 'if' efficiency savings are past on or as might be the case higher profits for cartel members.

The dissolving of the cartel results in the exposure of economic weakness within the individuals firms, after operating in a protected environment the inefficiencies come to the fore as highlighted by Aubert et al (2003) "There is almost universal agreement that price-fixing and market allocation cartels reduce economic efficiency." This reduction in efficiency can be shown in the firm and also it will impact on surrounding sector operations and political environments.

It is critical for the survival of the cartel structure that there is a secure and safe operating environment. Challenges to the organisation will weaken its position and open up opportunities for members to exploit co members weakness within the agreed operating parameters. The cartels key objective should be to ensure a stable market both in terms of political influence and consumer acceptability of supply and fixed price implementation. If all sides are content with the status quo then there is little motivation for cheating.

Utilities

The concept of state owned utilities is a post war structure that was devised to ensure the delivery of nationally required services that required significant amounts of infrastructure and investment.

The establishment of these natural monopolies enabled the mass take up of services and ensured the countries continued economic development. While the concept of state owned natural monopolies is a good way to 'kick start' large scale delivery infrastructure, the known inefficient operations of state owned firms means that the consumer s initial advantages from the organisation is reduced over a period of time due to a lack of structural investment and poor managerial ownership of the firms objectives.

Once the infrastructure as been established and there has been a return on the primary investment the option of de-nationalizing the organisation becomes a practical option. Examples of splitting these firms into infrastructure maintenance and service delivery have proven to be successful in some areas e.g. gas, electricity and telecoms. The competition to provide the consumer with a 'good deal' to encourage loyalty and attract new customers from competing firms means that prices offered should be lower that that of a state run monopoly simply on the basis of competition and the need to reduce costs for effective market place pricing. As Parker (1999) concludes "The main lesson is the way in which privatization with regulation can provide an environment in which former sleepy, state monopolies improve their economic performance to the benefit of both investors and consumers."

As most utility services are provided and established in most regions of Europe the move towards privatization within a loosely regulated framework would be a natural progression to allow more competitive pricing and a more consumer focused service delivery. This has been very evident in the de-regularization and privatization of telecom networks across Europe.

The merging and then nationalizing of smaller organisations to deliver nationally required infrastructure would allow for a more singular system of delivery with significant efficiency savings in construction. The risks to a national economy not ensuring standard delivery systems that are not connected are high, the resulting segmented development that would focus on major areas of population at the expense of more isolated elements of the community would restrict economic development. This is evident in the telecom sector where today large numbers of isolated communities are disenfranchised because of the lack of broadband access. This will impact on its development economically in our global trading where speed of transaction and information are 'king'. Even with the short comings in the private sector to accommodate isolated communities i am nor sure that a nationalized body would have been any better and maybe even worse at instigating the IT revolution.

There must be a balanced structure between infrastructure development and consumer value delivery. The old ways of State or Private operations must give way to a new structure of state and private partnership. It is only with the resources of the state and the innovation and efficiency of the private firm can any new national or international infrastructure system be effectively delivered to all members of our communities. So the question should not be about the old debate of pro and anti nationalization but about delivering a system that ensures all members of the community receive equal treatment and access.

NPV IRR

With project developments and product expansion the risks associate are varied and not always predictable, however there are strategies designed to assist the manager to reduce risk and hopefully enhance the organisations profits or service efficiently. Mechanisms employed to ascertain the best route for investment are varied but we shall explore the concepts of NPV and IRR as a starting point in the decision making process. Although these methods do not accommodate market risk and other non quantifiable elements that may impact of the outcome of the investment such as technological developments or associated hidden cost elements as pointed out by Anandarajan and Wen (1999). Baring in mind these short comings NPV and IRR when harmonious in conclusion can guide the decision make to asses on the appropriate course of action.

On an individual merit basis we can look at the resulting assessment of both NPV and IRR. To enable us to draw investment conclusions when there is not an harmonious outcome of calculations requires understanding of the differing input assumptions made when calculating each mechanism.

With NPV we calculate on the basis of the variation in present value of inward cash flow and that of present value cash outflow. The resulting decision from the results of the NPV calculations should take into account the vulnerability of future cash inflow.

Looking at IRR we calculate on the basis that future cash flows and the addition of the project or investment market value are equal or greater than the current value of the project.

Generally the two calculation mechanisms would give us a dual answer, however, when the answers are contradictory the process of deciding on a particular investment route becomes more subjective in many ways, while each system allows for particular inputs the future outcome is based on a certain amount of uncertainty which requires skilled interpretation using other external information and knowledge. The use of non academic theory plays a part in the decision making of the investment structural design when managers, entrepreneurs and executives embark on assessing investment criteria. This was identified by Graham and Harvey (2001) " financial executives are much less likely to follow the academically proscribed factors and theories when determining capital structure." However, when a conflicting set of data presents itself the decision maker is required to conclude an action of investment from only the data presented. In the NPV and IRR results the path chosen should account for certainty factor of the future cash inflows from the investment. If the resulting cash inflows are less than predicted then the resulting shortfall would impact on the IRR assumptions, therefore the option that i would derive a decision on would be the NPV result. This seem to be the favored route of most organisations as pointed out by Graham and Harvey (2001) it is reassuring that NPV is dramatically more important now as a project evaluation method than, as indicated in past surveys, it was 10 or 20 years ago.

While concluding that NVP would offer a more solid basis or even conservative decision on investment I do believe that using it as a sole basis is exposing the organisation to potential loss because of non awareness or consideration of market environmental factors.

Chapter 5

Finance Management

Introduction to management accounting

In a modern organisation the process of decision making for managers becomes less focused on intuition and experience and more focused on mechanisms that can evaluate and predict outcomes both in terms of cost and profit. Being able to assess a particular area or project with analysis that accommodates non financial and non tangible elements within its measuring elements then the resulting output is going to offer the manager greater flexibility and resource based decision making mechanisms that offer risk reduction and profit maximization While overviews of an organisations financial state may offer external viewers a broad perspective and financial 'photo fit' of the firm they do not drill down into the heart of the firm and evaluate the the structures and efficiencies of the organisation. This financial accounting process has served external audiences for many years and now only offers a fraction of the information that can be gleamed from data resulting from the more organic process of managerial accounting. By its very nature within the organisation it offers the viewer a much more realistic integration of the firms position as pointed out by Burns and Scapens (2000) "management accounting systems and practices stand between the structuring properties of institutions and the day-to-day actions and thoughts of organizational members"

To be able to assess a particular activity within a firm it becomes important to place the activity within a perspective that actively accounts for influences outside of the activity operating parameters. With traditional financial accounting there is no way of writing in influences and factors outside of the direct value inputs and outputs of the project. The resulting image is one that offers a clear clinical and stationary view of what could be a more vibrant and flexible activity . As a result the view projected from the financial accounting mechanisms does not realistic reflect the true status and potential of the project and leaves the manager short on sound decision making ground.

For better understanding of an activity and to allow more stoic decision making outcomes the process of managerial accounting can come into play and feed into the managers decision making mechanisms with a more solid base that allows and calculates for non financial impactors. The very free interpretation of data use and its ways of inclusion allow the manager to fully embrace the project in a way that the more regulated and myopic financial accounting systems does not allow.

Being able to facilitate decisions that allow contingency as is the case with management accounting systems means that the outcome is more adaptable and able to evolve through environmental changes. These more flexible and adaptable accounting systems will leave the manager more able to reach and enact more relevant and productive decisions. This was concluded by Chenhall and Morris (1986) "It is hoped that such approaches will enhance our abilities to understand what types of MAS are appropriate in different situations and, as a result, to improve the likelihood that MAS will help managers improve their performance and that of their organizations."

It is when variable factors and influences are not accommodated by management that is unaware or lacking in managerial accounting experience that the growth structure and profitability are negatively influenced. The firm will continue to operate but will be less able to react to market changes and place itself in and environment where it loses competitive advantage. Not using management accounting would not be the end of the firm but maybe the beginning of the end in a fast moving global market.

In conclusion we can see that managerial accounting meets the needs of a modern fast responding manager that requires a factual and flexible data assessments that accommodate subjective market and firm activity.

Burns & Scapens framework

Organizations always run the risk of establishing themselves into routines that are founded on historical activity. While this consistency may have had beneficial influence in the past, the current global market with more rapid response requirements means that traditional responses and solutions may not contribute to establishing competitive advantage. Methods and systems of delivering objectives that are established and routine may offer significant advantages in terms of establishing HR continuity and reduce the need for on going training, but they run the risk of blinding the firm to opportunity and advancement. We all tend to be resistant to change in some way and its manifestation within an organisation is a key element in the adoption of new practices and methods to enhance production output.

The Burns & Scapens framework described by Scapens (2006) explores the routines and rules of organisation and the concept that they dictate the actions and the understanding of actions within the collective organisation. Traditional actions and past decisions influence future decisions and actions. The historical lessons can play a major role in the progress or stagnation of an organisation. While commonality and familiarity in processes can establish firm operating grounds it can also impede development through lack of innovation. Scapens (2006) talks about lock-in and explains that decisions made in the past can drive and influence and to some degree restrict and modify decisions from the best to the most practical, resulting in a less efficient solutions. By constantly reviewing and comparing the interactions of actions, rules and routines management accounting can allow for a more complete analysis of the organisational functionality. This will allow for a more evolutionary approach to organisational change.

While Burns & Scapens (2006) suggest that management accounting change can be evolutionary or revolutionary, although primarily evolutionary Vaivio (1999) suggests "that change can also be conceived along the systematic and unsystematic dimension." Which ever approach we take the key element is going to be how we interact with those who are responsible for implementation and general acceptance of the change. Implementing change may result in resistance and only change that fits the concept of the organisations general culture of rules and routines will be implemented with any degree of success as pointed out by Kasurinen (2001) "only the implementation of the particular features which were in alignment with the institutionalized patterns of behavior in the organisation seemed to have succeeded." This commonality of operations once identified can be used to initiate change mechanisms for the implementation of new systems and actions.

The introduction of new systems and staff linked to traditional structures within the organisation needs to foster an atmosphere of trust. The lack of trust between key personnel in an organisation will endear it to resistance and potential failure when enacting change. There is a 'natural' mistrust of accountants when encompassed in a process of change. One of the key skills will be to identify when traditional actions need to be examined and changed. Getting the organisation out of a rut will lead to innovation and considerable advantage in achieving corporate goals.

Technological changes in operations and communication rapidity will influence and promote the concept and cause of management accounting. Bruggemann and Slagmulder (1995) highlight the view " it is argued that management accounting systems have to change when manufacturing technology changes". As system adapt and respond to the market forces in a way that staff and manages relate to on a daily basis then the mechanisms introduced will by their own results facilitate buy in. Organizations will embrace systems that meet the demands of modern global trading environment. The understanding that management accounting is more than number crunching is a critical element to selling the concept to 'non accountant' staff

Management accounting must meet the challenges of change in a way that empowers and enlightens individuals within the organisation to the advantages of system and process changes.

Any organisation will do well to review and analyze its habitual activity and asses its value within a globally focused organisation and market. The assessment of Scapens (2006) of management accounting change in new and established organisation show us that the human nature in group environments needs to be flexible and open to evolutionary change in the systems that dominate and impact on the decisions and actions we carry out on a daily basis. If this is the case and managers and personnel embrace management accounting change then organisations will hopefully perform in a more efficient and competitive manner. It is the human element that will play its part in successful change and as Granlund (2001) concluded "In order to secure meaningful and successful accounting system change it is not enough to concentrate on technical issues"

Costs

For organisational growth the concept of growing from historical activity is a path that is covered in danger. As with the risk of doing 'because we always have', decision making on historical data may not be relevant to current and future activity, therefore decisions should be made on data that is only directly relevant to the desired activity. Atrill & McLaney (2009) explain that historical costing factors should not influence the process of analyzing cost data in connection with future activity. The identification of relevant and non relevant costs plays an important role in reaching managerial decisions

The key arrears of costing decision mechanisms is to identify which costs available are relevant. Atrill & McLaney (2009) highlight the relationship between relevant and irrelevant costs by identifying relevant costs as Opportunity costs and future outlay costs that vary with the decision and the irrelevant costs as historical and future outlay costs that do not vary with the decision.

Defining the different elements and their time based relevance of cost data as follows will assist the manager in the decision making process.

Irrelevant Costs

Historical costs also identified as sunk or past costs that cannot change and therefore do not impact on the managers decision making mechanisms are identified as irrelevant. . Also when looking at future outlay costs it will be necessary to determine if those costs are variable to the decision made, if not then they are also deemed as irrelevant. Any cost that has previously been contracted will also not play a part in the mechanism of decision making.

Relevant Costs

To fully assess a project on the basis of costs it is important that those costs used have a determining element to the outcome of the decision and its variability. One such assessment is that of any opportunity costs attached to the project. Value attributed through known values through activity, actions and offers will need to be part of the judging system. Any future outlays costs that can vary with the outcome of the decision output characteristics should be evaluated and utilized in the decision.

The basis that past historic costs play no part in assessing new projects is not always a factor that is adopted by managers, reflecting on historical data seems to have a comforting factor for some. This is something that has been practiced in several organisations I have been involved in. The question "What did we pay last year or what are last years costs in comparison to this years?" as been a part of the costing process. Heath (1995) outlined the research that a large number of investors used past or sunk data in deciding future investment activity. Organizations must apply relevant process if they are to achieve more sustainable activities. While the instinct is to look back we must work towards processes in keeping with the framework outlined by Atrill & McLaney (2009). In my current position we are going through a significant analysis of our financial status due to the reduction in funding for NFP organisations and a reduction in commercial support from local businesses due to the fears and reality related to the current economic. Although my organisation is small and a not for profit community radio station the principles around looking at the real situation as opposed to the historical situation are now far more relevant and critical to the financial survival of the station.

In times of change the traditional use by some managers of using historical data is shown as being even less relevant than anticipated. It is a good time for more focused and relevant analysis along the lines shown by the assessment of Atrill & McLaney (2009) that will result in a better understanding of true costs and the implication towards a more profitable/efficient organisation.

In traditional approaches the supplier of a product would, in a limited or restricted market, aim to get the highest price possible for the product. Organizations strive for achieving profit maximization, however, achieving maximum price does not equate to a position of maximized profit. Being in a position of charging the highest price achievable exposes the organisation to the risk of alienating customers through a perceived over valuing of the product. While price is not always the deciding factor in purchasing actions, other factors such as rarity or desirability will play a crucial role. In order to achieve maximized return in in terms of financial profit it becomes critical for the firm to analyze the costs of production and endeavor to reduce costs at all levels to help achieve maximized profit. By focusing on the task of reducing costs and moving away from aiming for the highest functional price to firm opens up a larger potential market through lower retail pricing even though higher profits are achieved through cost control mechanisms. We will examine systems to assist managers gain higher returns through cost control and reduction systems.

The application of price fixing is a complex range of criteria that must avoid the risk of setting a price at the maximum level in the market environment. By setting a maximum level price will expose the firm to severe competition and run the risk of alienating customers by being viewed as exploitative.

Various costing mechanisms can be employed to ascertain a valid and competitive price. The skill for the manager is to identify the costing system suitable to the product environment. while traditional methods may approach the issue using a full costing method, however with organisations becoming larger and more diverse costing factors become more complex and far reaching, where smaller traditional localised firms had a more focused and relationship based view and understanding of costs, today the manager is faced with more disjointed cost data. This diverse cost based can be accounted for by utilizing Activity based costing mechanisms as described by Atril &McLaney (2009) although they do go on to identify that some firms believe that it is a "time consuming and costly" It is important to recognise that to achieve profit maximization there are 3 factors at play Costs, Volume and Prices as pointed out by Simon et al (n.d) Higher prices will not solely contribute to the maximization of profit.

By matching and applying the correct system of costing to achieve the most profitable pricing strategy is a task that needs to account for the environmental factors of the product acquisition. There only needs to be a cost allocation if the there is a symbiotic relationship between the department of the organisation and the product. Marginal costs factors would come into play in assisting the manager in determining price, however, other factors such as product positioning and competitive products. Pricing is not about cost plus scenarios, it is a complex mix of maths, economics, marketing and human nature.

We can see from the range of costing scenarios described by Atril &McLaney (2009) that the field is diverse and adaptable to the firms strategic planning. A firm should strive to charge the highest price for the market but not set a price that is above the level of acceptability for the consumer or target market. I strongly believe in the maxim that pricing is an evolutionary process, it will evolve to meet the market in a way that is sustainable or it will move the product to a position of extinction.

Budget Development

Developing budgets as directional guides and current status indicators for an organisation are a critical part of an organisations operating mechanisms, measurement and panning systems. The process of budget development is a vital part of the organisations operating priorities, it will define and point the firm into specific areas of operational activity and allow managers to measure the firms success in terms of a comparison measurements with the budget and the reality. How managers arrive at a realistic budget with organisational buy in is a critical process that must be based on as much factual data as possible and where required predicted data should be tampered to achievable rather than ambitious or unachievable figures. The application of fresh costing data and 'from the field' data from sales managers will help establish a close to reality picture in an ideal environment selected to apply the data. Unforeseen or variable activity should be adaptable within a budget. Knowing a firms inflows allows for assessment of outflows. The knowledge of potential sales allows for the development and establishment of outflow resources to meet predicted sales. One area that must be approached is the concept that the use of a budget is for future growth and innovation and not as an historical measuring stick, it is a future performance assessment mechanism.

The use of budget can serve several purposes including motivation, monitoring, controlling activities and responsibility assignment. The development and establishment of a budget that is based on the participation of budget controlling managers will require that managers understand that the figures generated must be realistic and not optimistic. Future sales should be based on market research and not rely on the concept of historical sales plus a bit more or less. If this data is used then the predicting of costs associated would flow more smoothly and be more adaptable if sales did not achieve their predicted level or did better than anticipated. Basing a budget without accounting for soundly based sales projections will leave a firm vulnerable to wide variances and unplanned activity. Adaptability in budgets is crucial for innovation and flexibility in a changing market as Becker and Green (1962) point out "Primarily, budgetary control has been the attempt to keep performance at or within the acceptable limits of the pre-determined flexible plan."

In my organisation we budget on the basis of predictive advertising sales figures, anticipated grant income and fund-raising activities. Some of these figures reflect historical activity but are increasingly based on market predictions. This is a result of discrepancies in budgets based on historical data and real situations in previous years. This is more prominent in the current economic environment where operational and financial influencers differ from recent years.

The need to have and react to real situations dictates that as close as possible real data should be employed in deriving budgets. This 'close to' real data should come from and be based on potential income for the firm. Costs associated with, and adaptable to changes in these sales, can then be derived. I would conclude that deriving budgets from projected sales data would allow for a more adaptable and manageable budgeting system that would allow for a more realistic buy in from organisational members. Budgets must by their very nature be adaptable to variations in the realistic data compared to the predicted data. Budgets and the methods used to reach them should be transparent as concluded by Alesina and Perotti (1996) even though they where talking about state budgetary requirements I believe this applies to organisations. This enables buy in and understanding of targets and associated cost which lead to better motivation and productivity as described by Atrill and Mclaney (2009).

Balanced Scorecard

The need for an organisation to anticipate required actions and activity in future market participation requires a balanced approach that can draw on historical financial data and its forward projections, however, successful organisations need to be able to fully asses data and trends for future activity. This blending of historical and future predictive activity will enable a firm to better understand the environment it is participating in. Being able to solidify corporate vision and strategy through a defined process of assessment such as a Balanced Scorecard approach is a way of consolidating issues and direction. This is defined by Nerreklit (2000)The scorecard translates the vision and strategy of a business unit into objectives and measures in four different areas: the financial, customer, internal-business-process and learning and growth perspectives. By fully understanding these areas of evaluation a firm can develop its key targets and objective. A process that is a fundamental activity for the achievement of competitive advantage and profit maximization through efficient organisation practice.

The concept of Balanced Scorecard is to take a strategy and develop and implement an operational process. If we break this down into the 4 key areas developed by Kaplan and Norton as illustrated by Atrill and Mclaney (2009) we can measure specific data specific to the key area of Finance, Customer, Internal business process and learning and growth.

The understanding of issues and activity in these areas is a fundamental driver towards successful operations. While the process does not prescribe objectives for the firm it sets the course on developing the sound and functional objectives through situational understanding. By taking a vision and strategy and assessing each key area in terms of objective, Measures, Targets and Initiatives managers will understand the functional activity of the organisations departments and then be able to relate and encompass those situations in to a corporate direction. By utalising this method a manager is able to capture data that is both internal and external along with historical and predictive, giving a more balanced approach to defining current and future firm and market actions. The mechanisms can also be used to asses the position and actions of an organisation as part of an internal review and performance assessment. Simply understanding the position of a particular department can direct the corporation in a better and more efficient direction. Information is a key to success and the balanced scorecard is one of the methods of improving communication as pointed out by Martinsons et al (1999).

Employing the balanced scorecard system to an organisation is something I have not taken part in, however, I can see the advantages as I have always been of the opinion that future actions are not about past actions but about learning and enhancing knowledge. This is a system that can assist managers to focus and perform on operational issues and not be looking for action justification on an ad hoc basis. Structured introduction into even the smallest firm will give managers the key to unlocking the correct door to future activity. While the format of the balance scorecard has been defined there is no reason for modifications to be made to suit differing circumstances as done by Tesco and highlighted by Atrill and Mclaney (2009). Used as an ongoing measurement system it serves to focus and measure activity in a flexible and operationally focus manner.

We can see that the Balanced Scorecard is a flexible and informative method of assessing activity and directing future operations to meet the strategic objectives of the firm. The framework is becoming more common and will be adapted and focused by organisations as time passes, ensuring that managers get a more helpful tool in monitoring and developing activity that does not just measure performance on historical financial data.

NPV

When managers need to review and decide on an investment path there are several mechanisms that could be employed. The justification of actions needs to be based on a range of data other than straight financial measuring, however, financial data will play a critical part in the measurement and decision path. To this end the manager needs to evaluate alternative placement of funds as a measurement comparison over a period of time. Time frame will play a major role in the calculation of aiming to achieve a true value of an investment. When time is a critical factor in evaluating investment actions it is the NPV mechanism that would be used to reach time discounted value data. NPV plays a significant role over the more simplistic systems such as ARR and PP.

If we are to value and evaluate an investment at any given time then we need to account for factors that would impact on the decision making process and the timeframe in which those decisions are relating to. Accounting for any potential loss from alternative investments will play a role along with the risk exposure and any inflationary impact as highlighted by Atrill and Mclaney (2009). The mechanism of discounting over time gives the manager a more realistic view of the investment project at any given time and allow for more sound financial assessment. As the prime objective of any investment is going to be the increase of the investors wealth then this ability to place the investment in terms of now NPV is going to be a favorable tool for managers to facilitate. Having a real value formulated by the NPV method offers a more realistic overview of the investment that is only determined as percentages in other mechanisms that only look at financial data that is a direct fixed environment factor that does not accommodate the impact of timing, risk and inflationary factors.

NPV is not a method I have employed in any of my activities but I can see that in looking at investment projections over variable time periods it is a valuable tool in the assessment of projects and their potential financial value. This is something that I will be exploring further and comparing with the PP method used by most of the projects I have been involved with. Applying NPV within the organisations assessment and valuation activities will become a more standard tool as organisations embark on more long term investment strategies.

In conclusion I would recommend that the use of NPV becomes a critical element of assessing investment for organisations long term development strategies. Although there still seems to be resistance to moving to NPV as discussed by Shapira and Shaver (2009). When looking at short term projects the use of NPV will not play a major role in the decision making process as the key influencing factors will play a less influential role in the return of the investment.

Setting Transfer Prices.

Product movement across large organisations needs to be transferred and financially accounted for to help ensure efficient functioning and real situation costing. By utalising transfer pricing methodology an organisation can transfer fiscal responsibility for a product from one division to another. As Atrill and Mclaney (2009) illustrate the key objectives for transfer pricing are: Allocation of divisional resources, Taxation efficiency, divisional independence, performance measurement and optimization of profits. With these key objectives managers can work towards delivering on profit maximization and competitive advantage for the firm, however, an individual manager can jeopardize the success of the company by acting in a way that benefits the division over the firm or because individual objectives benefit the manger over the firm. This potential conflict of interest should be monitored and addressed by all organisations that operate a transfer pricing system. This problem was highlighted by Holstrom & Tirole (1991) We have implicitly assumed that the divisional managers are short-terra players. Of course, if they can themselves develop reputations for being fair (i.e., (applying quality and paying their trading partner adequately for quality), then much of the transfer pricing problem may disappear.

The mechanisms for the effective establishment of transfer pricing are based of several method and can be utilized by the organisation for the most profitable and organizationally sustainable outcome. We have seen that internal pricing is just as critical as external price setting. The 'knock on' effect of poor price setting can impact across the entire organisation and influence levels of profitability and efficiency. Setting out to establish the selling price can be based on various price indicators including Market Price, Variable cost, Full Cost and Negotiated price. When it comes to pricing product or services for internal / inter divisional purposes Atrill and Mclaney (2009) suggest that the calculations be made on the principle of opportunity cost. This, when operating in an ideal trading environment may offer the better solution, however, the price may on occasions be higher than external sources. This conflict would leave the manage in a difficult purchasing dilemma with serious ramifications to the organisations and divisions profitability. All of these can be used by managers in determining the selling price and the strategy chosen is going in most cases be a matter of organisational policy.

Applying one or some of the above mechanisms to ascertain the best selling price for inter organisation transactions is going to be influenced by the methods adopted and the objectives to price setting.Where a company uses transfer pricing as a means of tax efficiency then it must be aware that there will be comparative transaction analyses carried out to determine its validity as prescribed by the OECD as illustrated by Gresik & Osmundsen (2008). Other objectives for implementing a transfer pricing policy for the organisation may well improve the ownership of activity within the supply chain and final product. One method of achieving ownership of transaction between divisions is through negotiated price setting. This means that the risk of an individual manipulating prices for personal gain is reduced and a more 'entire process' related price can be achieved.

The use of and the methods employed in establishing a transfer price is going to depend on the reasoning for using such mechanisms. Tax implications can be a serious motivator in international trade and if the act of fiscal movement can enhance the shareholder wealth then organisations are going to embark on such activity. To use such systems for organisational efficiency and inter-department responsibility and accountability is a sound basis for organisational development and sustainability.

Inventories

Organizations striving to operate at maximum efficiency need to asses their levels of inventories. Determine holding so that neither customer satisfaction are impaired and organisational costs are maintained at the most economically acceptable levels. The management of inventories is a simple task when sales levels are known and supplies are stable, unfortunately the commercial environment does not behave in such a stable and predictable manner. Variances in demand and seasonal demand fluctuations need to be accounted for and forward projections calculated and levels set to accommodate customer need. The key to successful inventory management was highlighted by Nenes, Panagiotidou, & Tagaras (2010) The desired solution is a suitable inventory control policy that will guarantee a satisfactory service level without keeping unnecessarily large inventories that are costly and difficult to handle. This balancing act is just as vital in a small scale business as a large international operation. Managers responsible for ensuring the 'on demand' supply of the organisations products must utilize all available sources of information to ensure the maintenance of supply chains to the customer.

The management of data to asses current and future stoke levels can impact on a managers ordering of raw materials and the assignment of production capacity when trying to achieve optimum levels of inventory. Some decisions may require buying raw material forward such as aviation fuel in the airline industry (MRP). This strategy means that levels of future fuel prices will impact on how economically influenced the organisation is in terms of pricing and cash-flow If market prices increase then the airline is in a favorable economic position and it fuel holdings are a positive for the firm, a decrease in price then the situation is reversed. When there is a change in travel trends that results in a fall in demand, such as the 9/11 events, when demand for air travel dropped airlines are left with surplus inventories of fuel and aircraft. While such dramatic events are out of the predictive scope of organisations they do show how inventory holdings need to be adaptable and have value outside of normal supply chains. As Atrill & McLaney (2009) illustrate inventory levels carry implications on costs attributed to holding, handling and storing of raw materials and product. The surplus levels of inventory will impact on profitability.

I have experienced the dilemma of trying to predict future movements in aviation fuel and our requirements to forward purchase. The levels held by airlines can impact seriously on the ticket pricing strategy if the firms purchasing and inventory holding strategy is out of sync with market movement.

The fine balance between future demand and financial prudence when setting levels is a skilled task that can influence the future credibility and profitability of the firm. The management of the resulting levels of inventories must be monitored and any fluctuations to predicted movement must be flagged and strategies employed to ensure continued supply to customers and maintain profitability for the firm. The over stocking will restrict the amount of working capital for the firm and impact on cash-flow The management of inventories is a critical element of ensuring competitive advantage and profit maximization

Chapter 6

Management in a multicultural Context

Global Environment

Local to Global – Making sense of each other.

Rapid exchange of information and the increasing rate of across the globe trade offers the world an opportunity to create a growing level of personal and cultural understanding and tolerance. Trade maybe the key to some of the serious issues that separate us as nations and individuals. While the barriers to harmonious existence are a challenge to us and future generations the new breakthroughs in delivering media around the world and simplification of travel will enhance understanding and develop tolerance. While this may seem idealistic in its approach the power of commerce can be a great influencer. Rapid communication allows a greater opportunity for negotiation and mutual settlement. As organisations grow and with the reduction in trade and employment restrictions we will be exposed more and more to new operating environments based on the political and cultural diversity of the nations and people we interact with. How we translate these multi cultural work place environments into fully functioning profitable efficient organisational entities is going to be key.

Globalization is as pointed out by Mead & Andrews (2009) at risk of becoming a cliche. It is many things to many people and to encapsulate it as a single defined situation runs the risk of over simplification and misunderstanding. In its most negative incarnations it can be seen as large conglomerate organisations exploiting and destroying smaller firms, nations and environments. This along with fixed almost imperialistic attitudes will only foster negative responses from countries being entered and create a restrictive environment. To fully capitalize on the opportunities of globalization, in it broadest sense organisations, must learn to integrate and accept the differences in attitudes, work pattens and approaches. By implementing policies of integration and social inclusion with in the management of the organisation and its work force firms will be able to more efficiently understand and exploit new markets around the world . From the expansion of the larger globalised organisation we can see the re-emergence of local culture and tradition, although there is a risk that these smaller localised activities could be highjacked and exploited we must understand that culture and tradition is the changing face of our environment.

Working in a multinational and multicultural environment is at times invigorating and frustrating. The frustration is born of misunderstanding and possibly non intentional prejudice. When I was working with a start up low cost airline in Spain a few years ago I had not only to adapt to a different culture of state bureaucracy and work place practices I also had a multinational team of managers and investors. The art of understanding underlining meaning, issues of language, our office was a mixture of English, Spanish, Swedish, German, Polish, Creol and Arabic, although English was the 'official' language, a strategic choice rather than cultural, this approach as been identified by Luo and Shenkar (2006) Unlike national culture, language is a strategic choice, however, embedded in culture and evolving institutional realities. The reality here was all staff spoke English and all international communications and contracts where in English, even though internal communication could sometimes breakdown. The solution was simple, all key communications were recorded between individuals and departments. (In English). Differing views of humor was also an interesting element and potential conflict area although there was a collective understanding of differences and attempts to 'understand' the different approaches to what was perceived to be funny.To fully appreciate the potential of global organisations the opportunity to work with such a large group from such diverse background was a true education and one I treasure.

There maybe may classifications of the term globalization and its implementation but the fundamentals of a world that interacts and exchanges goods, information, ideas and beliefs is one that will stand the test of time. We must not use globalization as a means to exploit the weak or the disenfranchised, as managers we have a responsibility to empower our fellow workers and maximise on the opportunity of global wealth generation. Managing on a global scale requires managers to listen and learn new ways of motivating people from varying backgrounds and communicating the organisations vision in ways that cross boundaries and concepts. As Ely and Thomas (2001) conclude cultural diversity is a potentially valuable resource that the organization can use, not only at its margins,to gain entree into previously inaccessible niche markets, but at its core, to rethink and reconfigure its primary tasks as well.

Political Culture or Branding Culture?

Successful globalised economic transactions and international social interactions are governed by the acceptable behavior and understanding of the communicating parties. In the so called global culture we assume that the standardization of understanding is going to reduce conflict and confusion within corporate and political environments. It is important to evaluate concepts and frameworks that address differing approaches and interpretation of cultural dynamics. The postulation that nations can function with a sound and diverse set of cultural meanings that can be modified or compromised to meet the needs of the majority and move the nation to a common goal is a foundation for success in an idealistic manner. As Chevrier (2009) explores the idea that national culture is not based 'shared values' but on a collective understanding of 'national political culture'. It is important to consider the dangers of such cultural compromise and the longterm impact of the nation and organisation. While organisations can, if required, employ on the basis of employee 'blend in' strategy. Nations are less flexible and at risk of isolating and disenfranchising minorities who function on differing believe and cultural ideals. The concept that a nation can function as a large organization based on homogenous standards and believes is to threaten the fabric of human social development. Culture is a tool to global understanding and as such should be embraced as a means of development and not sterilized for the 'national standard brand'. While nations may share values in terms of legal and social construction the strength of a nation comes from the acceptance of differing cultures and the harvesting of concepts and activities that benefit national and global development.

Nations and organisations are generally comprised of a multi cultural structure and need to function effectively. To achieve an efficient operation there will need to be an evolutionary acceptance process towards cultural messages within the organisation or state. Imposition of cultural change is deemed to risk failure when the new 'cultural values' are conflicting with current values and frameworks. This was described by Boddy (2008) who explains that managers should be aware and take account of sub cultures within the organization, nations should also account for sub cultural influence.

When studying culture in a management context we should not lose sight of the anthropological elements and theories to culture. The assumption that environment influences culture should be explored by managers and leaders when defining strategy and policy. As Bird and Fang (2009) point out "Environment makes a difference in thinking and behavior" How we deal or perceive differing concepts in terms of culture was explored by Martin (2002) as explained by Boddy (2009). The observer should view culture from one of three perspectives. 1.Integration – focusing on consistencies. 2. Differentiation – focusing on conflict. 3. Fragmentation – Focus on the interplay and change of views. By employing one or all of the perspectives a manager can build a better understanding of the underlining cultural feeling of the organisation. This could very well apply to the construction of social policy at state level.

By delivering a cultural approach that is based on the concept of national political culture risks reducing culture to a set of clinical strap lines and passionless structure. To fully capture the diverse believes, behaviors and drivers of a multi cultural society we must embrace common ground, accept differences and understand that culture is a fluid and transient state that evolves with the very people who practice its traditions. Chevrier (2009) approach while in many ways offers a 'globalised' solution it does encapsulate the perception that globalization is about standardization. If globalization is going to work we should strife towards constructing cultural concepts and development around the perspective approach described earlier. This will empower sub culture and give the mainstream opportunities to optimize behavior and strategy to meet the needs of all. Using a national political cultural concept will weaken managers ability to truly appraise process and implementation of strategy and action because the homogenized standards will not reflect underlining influencers from disenfranchised sub cultures both internally and externally. The only true route for valid appraisal and implementation is through exploration and understanding of cultural drivers. Chevrier (2009) seems to miss the influence of sub culture structure and influence. In national policy making the use of political culture should be used as an assessment tool in the managers tool box this is supported by Elkins and Simeon (1979) who suggest that Political culture should seldom be seen as competing with other variables, but as a complement to them. Only if the political culture concept is to be any use, it is as a way to gain a broad overview that allows further exploration and sub cultural discovery.

Undermined Culture

Before todays globalization cultures could stand alone and develop and evolve at a pace the was culturally acceptable. Information inputs where at lower levels and external social and cultural norms were less readily available. This cultural isolation is now, accept in very rare cases, a thing of the past. We are all faced with the opportunity and reality of coming face to face with differing cultures. These culture interactions will result in possible 'cross pollination' of attitudes, practices and believes. The media will play a major role in exposing people to new concepts of behavior, responsibility, social and individual interactions. In many ways this exposure will assist the manager in understanding the complexity of cross cultural interactions. Of course, all of this media distribution of culturally provoked activity and foundations may well introduce new elements into more traditional sectors of society and implement the rapid evolution of cultural trends and lifestyles. We have seen the rapid deployment of fast food outlets around the world and their influence to change the eating habits of entire nations. While this may only be perceived as a surface change and could be argued that 'core' values will remain steadfast, the possibility is there to actively influence cultural change. In terms of human rights, many changes have been made internationally as to what is and what isn't acceptable even when some actions were seen as 'cultural'. All of these changes will make it more difficult to do comparative analysis on cultures as they become more 'polluted'. In relation to changes in political structure there will also follow changes in cultural behavior and values as Inglehart and Baker (2000) pointed out when referring to the downfall of Communism "we predict that they will move toward modern and post industrial values in the new millennium."

Even if culture is evolving at a more rapid rate than it would have done without the influence of media and the development of technological communication systems it is still vital to analyst cultural foundations and how that 'fits' the globalization template. Moving away from national stereotyping and approaching cultural interactions on the basis of establishing harmony as proposed by Trompenaars and Hampden-Turner (1997) and highlighted by Mead and Andrews (2009) is a way of combating cultural dilemma and misunderstanding. The approach of dealing with frameworks proposed by Trompenaars on an interactive individuals interactions and influences with culture would sit more comfortably in a rapidly changing global cultural environment. Understanding the positioning of individuals within cultural structures is a valuable tool for managers and organisations that will allow internal strategic development and also allow for greater global market penetration.

We can best reflect the global cultural changes in terms of food. The internalization of food shows that barriers to cultural experiences are dropping. Today we can accept that Indian, Asian, American, African and European food is part of the UK diet. If we accept food influences then we will move on in time to really asses values and behaviors from differing cultures. This growing willingness to explore will allow managers the flexibility and strength to offer differing work practices and attitudes to the work force, although they will probably be adapted to blend with the 'home' culture. Managers must see themselves as Ambassadors to cultural understanding within their organisations.

With a diverse cultural base in the global organisation there is a need to embrace policies that promote inclusion and acceptance. It should become part of our global culture to value and promote culture in all its forms. Protect the past but adapt and improve where possible as Griswold (1999) concluded "A culture that changes does not lose its identity just because it is changing."

Individual, social and organisational value changes through cross-convergence.

Individuals go through life learning and changing ideas, views and perspectives of the world around them. Collecting and adapting opinions of others and evolving personal concepts and positions is an on going practice for most people. These fluctuations can be initiated by various stimuli that relate to the persons environment and activities. Our views opinions and understanding of the world is very different at the age of 16 compared to those of when we are say 50. These changes are a direct result of personal experiences and learning. In the same way as the individual evolves different values so the collective can move in similar ways. Sharing information and adapting others views, concepts and beliefs in to our personal value structures can manifest itself in the larger cultural environment.

The factors that determine changes in values have been described by Ralston (2008) as sociocultural, economic, political and technological. All of these categories can influence the individual and the organisation. If we look at the theory of cross-convergence, that is the influence of social cultural and business ideology into new value structures. This becomes a stronger influencer within a globally operating organisation. Diverse cultural values throughout organisations in various cultural environments expose all individuals to varying cultural views and this may result in individual value or believe modification.

Looking at cross-convergence and cultural tendencies as descried by Kelley et al (2005) we can see that culture is not static but an evolutionary organism. The evidence from their study maybe weighted because of the relationship between Hong Kong and the UK being culturally bonded by historical ties, however, adaptability in social and business communication and value sharing tendencies is going to have varying degrees of view molding depending on the original divergence of the original values.

Ralston (2008) as proposed that there are three categories described as: conforming crossvergence, static cross-vergence and deviating crossvergence. This enhancement of the cross-convergence theory shows that the movement of values is complex and not a narrowly prescribed process of evolution but a collection of influencing factors based on perspective orientation and value starting points.

Values and attitudes in the work place can be diverse both influenced through social and organisational cultural standpoints. The encapsulating environment of the workplace requires a common operating point in terms of values and attitudes. At some point the corporate developed internal operational policies will impact on social activities. Looking at social interactions within the workplace that is governed by corporate culture and then on a non corporate social situation will see values and attitudes applied outside of the organisations environment. One such area that is open to value conflict is the amount of time one is required to work within the organisation. Perspectives on acceptable 'work ethic' will raise conflict when the national culture as a predisposition to fewer working hours than say a new MNE that expects staff to commit to the organisation in terms of extra time. Stier & Lewin-Epstein (2003) found that "A clear preference for increasing time spent on work is evident in former socialist countries (especially Russia and Bulgaria), and Mediterranean countries such as Spain and Israel. The proportion preferring to devote more time to work activity is lowest in developed countries such as Sweden, Japan, the United Kingdom, and France" This potential conflict will need to be managed where there is conflict between social value and organisational value to work ethic. A situation that may well result an evolutionary solution towards a balanced productivity assessment. Output would be the measure rather than hours worked, a change in value and attitude by both organisation and staff (sociocultural). Such changes are common in our changing and globalising environments. We can see that attitudes to women in the work place have changed in recent years, even though some would say that 'glass ceilings' may still exist. Attitude changes toward women developed in the work place transfer to the social environment and empower women socially.

We are all functioning in fluid environments that take cultural information from many sources, media, social and business. To say that we are immune to this information would be foolhardy, we are influenced at all levels and those influence will educate and inform our values and beliefs. This is also the case with culture, it can never be static and must adapt and transform to accommodate changing environments and external interactions.

Negotiating in a multicultural environment.

The art and psychology of negotiating is a skill that needs to be continually developed and refined by international managers. There has been a large amount of literature regarding the protocols and techniques of international negotiations, resulting in the need for more sophisticated interactions. Assuming that the parties involved have established an understanding of the cultural aspects then how best to use that knowledge and integrate it into achieving key objectives is paramount. Planning is going to be the driver of negotiations, especially in an international context.

Understanding the culture of both the organisation and nation are vital along with the establishment of grounded relationships between all negotiators. Of course approaches to negotiating will vary depending on the reason for negotiation whether conflict resolution or the formation of new business transactions. Approaches to talks will vary depending on the cultural perspective towards deal brokering, some cultures would embark on a slow trust building and getting to know you process while others would be more direct and defined from the outset. Which ever approach is used the negotiations can, on a basic level, be defined as either distributive or Integrative as described by Metcalf et al

(2007). Using the distributive concept will require one side to 'give up' and could be conceived as a more confrontational approach. Integrative style would allow for a richer more solution bound approach that benefits all parties. Successfully completing negotiations will require clear methods of communication, both verbal and non verbal, something that can be difficult to achieve across cultures and language. Careful consideration must be placed on who will carry out the process. Mead and Andrews (2009). It is important that mangers enter the negotiating arena in a position that 'demands' respect from the opposing team, issues such as age, corporate status and possibly gender would need to be considered. Creating the right image at the table will ensure a smooth start. Once the visual profile is established the negotiator will need a range of skills such as those defined by Hurn (2007) listening skills; sensitivity to cultural differences; orientation towards people; willingness to use team assistance; high self-esteem; high aspirations; and attractive (i.e. people-orientated) personality. All of these delivered in a culturally acceptable manner would lead a potentially successful outcome assuming that key objectives are attainable. During the process of multi cultural discussions it is important that tolerance and patients is required along with acceptance of differing ways and not taking offense if the opposing party make a cultural 'faux pas'.

On a couple of occasions in Spain I was talking to several bodies regarding the operational base of a new airline. On at least two separate incidents the people we were talking with arrived very late for a meeting with no apology or explanation. Thinking this was a negotiating ploy designed to make us feel unimportant I withdrew from the meeting 'deeply offended' Of course later I learned that this was normal practice with no implied meaning so I adapted my approach. I was operating on a monochromic basis and the other party where acting in a polychromic manner as Hurn (2007) illustrates. Simple misunderstandings based on our own cultural expectations can damage negotiations.

Critical to successful negotiating is the ability to use and understand the values and traditions of your opposing colleagues as part of the negotiating strategy. Developing a sound personal relationships will play a vital part of the process, even if operating in a more individualist environment. Understanding and communication combined with clear goals will enable a successful outcomes, nobody enters negotiations to walk away without a deal.

Communicating across boundaries for competitive advantage -

Getting the message across.

Developing and motivating teams in a virtual environment requires differing skill sets and ethical leadership standards for managers. Operating in a more disjointed and impersonal 'virtual office' environment will involve greater pressure on managers to monitor and evaluate actions and activities of team members. Globalization and technology developments have meant that the way in which organisations communicate needs to be evaluated and developed to ensure competitive advantage is achieved. Issues of communication and management procedure over geographic and cultural boundaries has raised the bar in terms of a managers skill and understanding of functioning in a multinational environment. The global environment today is a rapidly chancing face that requires fast innovative responses to an ever changing market. Communication and the management of trans national and inter organisational teams requires the establishment sound trust and individual responsibility based on management approaches that promotes a collective acknowledgment of individual project or element ownership. Operating a culturally diverse team requires a solid universal level of communication that encourages all aspects of culturally based ideas and concepts within an open, exploratory and innovative manner. This type of environment will foster progress and ensure the organisation achieves competitive advantage across market sectors. This is highlighted by Lee (2009) when explaining Kant's ethical guidelines emphasize a universal standard of behavior whereby individuals are treated with respect and never exploited as a means to an end. A true team will function as a collective but within an environment of individual responsibility.

Working towards enacting a multi-cultural, trans global virtual team requires the establishment of e-ethical standards of operation and communication protocols that account for the multi lingual diversity of the team. As not all members of the team would have the same first language the importance of structuring communication of data and concepts must be based on the language skills of the team and account for the potential issues of cultural and language miss-interpretation of thoughts and comments.

Leading a virtual team in a manner that accounts for the e-ethical issues such as communication strategies, risk management, resource management and goal setting will require the ability to express and explain in a manner that encourages 'buy in' and facilitates smooth management processes. The leadership established functioning of the team is a critical part of success. Lee (2009) General management literature shows that the manager's leadership style and competence has a direct and measurable impact on the organization's performance. When a manager instills their leadership within a virtual team in a manner that fully communicates and controls e-ethical issues then levels of efficiency and motivation will improve. As Symons & Stenzel (2007) states Human communication is an important aspect of virtual teaming.

The establishment of clear ground rules in how the virtual team operates is critical to good, effective distance communication and project fulfillment. Weaknesses in how messages, decisions and concepts are delivered will foster conflict through misunderstanding and fear. I currently chair a national organisation that represents and lobbies for community media in Ireland. We have functioned very well in a semi virtual manner for a long time, until recently. We had a couple of new members elected to our board and we suddenly find ourselves not delivering on key targets because of poor communication and the resulting mis trust. This was simply down to the fact that the original team functioned on established levels of individual responsibility and trust based on long standing working relationships. The new members did not have that bonded approach and therefore felt disenfranchised from the original group. We have of course worked to bring into the fold through increased sharing of task based information and protocol confirmation. The group is a diverse collection of people from differing organisational cultures. In a multi national cultural group this would have been a lot more problematic to resolve because of language and cultural differences and it only emphasizes the need to establish clear lines and protocols of communications. Brett et al (2006) tells us that Multicultural teams often generate frustrating management dilemmas. Cultural differences can create substantial obstacles to effective teamwork .

Operating in a culturally diverse team across the globe can, providing communications are universal, lead to competitive advantage because of the variety of cultural understanding within differing markets. This leads to innovative lines of development and implementation actions. Keeping the human element in team management is even more critical when operating through technology across time, geographic and cultural boundaries.

Virtual cross cultural team development – Best practice

Ensuring smooth effective operations across multi national markets requires the establishment of teams that can understand and capture market trends in diverse cultural and political environments. The multi national enterprise (MNE) must utilize communication skills and practices in a multi cultural virtual teams in order to establish competitive advantage in it culturally diverse target markets at the most efficient and profitable manner possible. Managers empowered to operate teams that span cultures and language differences must ensure that all team members abide to a defined set of communication processes, protocols and recognise the cultural and language differences within the team. Recognizing these differences will allow the development of a symbiotic body that works in harmony towards a common goal. This paper will work through some of the issues faced by a manager when forming and managing a cross cultural team that functions in a virtual environment across the globe.

Challenges

The manager of a cross cultural team will face additional challenges above those of ensuring the delivery of the firms goals. The team manager will need to demonstrate key leadership / visionary abilities along with a practical approach to administering culturally and geographically diverse teams.

The following aspects where defined by Zakaria et al (2004) as some of the challenges faced by organisations when developing cross cultural virtual teams:

Creating effective team leadership

Managing conflict and global virtual teams dynamics

Developing trust and relationships

Understanding cross-cultural differences

Developing intercultural communication competence

When these challenges are recognized mangers can move towards implementing operational mechanisms that account for and avoid possible negative outcomes. When communications are in harmony with the diversity of cultural influences the team will begin to function efficiently.

Representation

How a team is represented and functions is going to be critical to its success. Choosing an operational standard environment, in terms of cultural make up and managerial processes, will be the key driver for the organisation. Issues as to whether the structure should be culture specific or cross cultural will depend on the diversity of the target market and the human resource make up of the organisation.

Cultural specific foundations.

For the organisation to embark on a strategy of culturally specific make up will allow for smoother communications between team members but may very well create a delivery process that is biased and mismatched to the target market when it is not within the cultural understanding of the team. This type of situation can arrive when a firm is entering new markets utalising is home based employee base. The advantage of creating a cultural specific team is seen when it is matched to the target market, although there may be mismatched communications with the home based staff leading to potential non alinement of regional and organisational strategies.

Cross cultural foundations.

The establishment of a team based on a wide range of cultural perspectives will better place the organisation to operate on an inter regional and national basis. The team would have a wide over view of differing markets and with the sharing of culturally specific data from members of the team harmonization of organisational strategy can be achieved at a high level of efficiency.

Human Resource Implications

When appointing teams that function across borders there needs to be a strategic approach to recruitment that matches the strategic objectives of the firm. The organisation can approach the recruitment in terms of a staff – task matching process. This could utilize several styles of management and team structure that includes ethnocentric, polycentric or geocentric strategies. Choosing an approach is a difficult task that must account for numerous factors within the operational and functional efficiency of the organisations targets and goals. Marchhington &Wilkinson (2008) determine that "it is sometimes difficult to determine which approach might suit organisational circumstances because so much depends on the availability of managers who possess appropriate qualities" Once a team is established how it relates to other organisations within in its communication range will need to be determined. The interaction internally may differ from that of certain external bodies as there may need to be a more culturally sympathetic approach to achieve goals. Just as bi or multi lingual skills may be advantageous it must also be recognized that a team that demonstrates bi or multi cultural communication skills will achieve more.

Best Practice Model

Conventual meetings function under various social functions that include pre and post meeting conversations combined with food and drink. This allows for relationships to develop, something that does not occur when communications and meetings are carried out over geographic and time differences.

Changes in communication actions in meetings will require a different set of operating parameters to account for the lack of visual communication indicators. A defined set of audio conferences protocols are critical, knowing when and how to enter conversations, enter and leave the forum and clarify comments that are not fully understood. This is confirmed by Bal and Foster (2000) A set of checklists and best practices is essential to guide team members throughout the meeting, e.g. an agreed method for entering and leaving the discussion.

Designing a set of best practices should be devised by the team to allow ownership and start to create working relationships.

We can see that the mix and make up of an firms team is going to play a major role in its success. The choices made by managers in recruiting and establishing protocols is best carried out in a manner that compliments the operational culture of the organisation. If the firm is moving into a global market then it must strive to recruit a culturally diverse team and not rely on a mono culture derived from its own resources. Firms should expand its HR base when embarking on global operations in order to achieve market specific competitive advantage.

Designing a way to speak: Communicating across the language divide.

Even when two people from the same language and cultural background enter into a communication process misunderstanding and conceptual issues can arise from poor communicating structure. Key to that structure is going to be the context in which messages are related. When an organisation establishes itself in different language and cultural environments it needs to set out clear structure and protocols on both verbal and written communication processes in order to maintain the contextual structure in relation to the organisations overhaul strategic objectives. Language misunderstanding and implied meanings are potential barriers to successful global strategies, both internally and externally to the organisation. It becomes imperative that all members of the organisation communicate from a broad understanding of how messages, concepts and vision are structured for efficient understanding and with reduced risk of miscommunication. If all are operating at the same perceptive level then breakdowns are going to occur less frequently and smoother movement toward objectives will be seen.

Avoiding misunderstanding and offense is a paramount objective in establishing internal and external communications for the global organisation. Operating in one language may be preferential but it will deliver issues for localised operations where the organisations communication language is not the language of the operating environment. Transferring messages needs to be clear and not structured in a way that reflects the cultural background of the writer. This more clinical approach to communication can reduce the impact of message importance, especially where vision and motivation are the key objectives, but it will reduce the risk of offense and misunderstanding within the staff. Internally it is easier to establish protocols to meet the objectives of smoother communications. Language design for an organisation is a critical part of its international communication strategy. Saying what you want to say is one thing, saying it so that all the receivers of the message understand it is yet another. How organisations develop their language protocols will depend on various elements of the firms objectives and structure. This is highlighted by Lou and Shenkar (2006) global language design is shaped by international strategy, organizational structure, and level of trans-nationality.

When looking at examples of potential miscommunication such as that described by Oososthuiz (2004) and its catastrophic potential in the realms of internal and external communication we can understand the need to use language design in an intelligent manner that accommodates the evolutionary nature of global organisations. Our experiences of religious, political and social up bringing will impact on how we structure our messages, this combined with our world understanding through media exposure will give us tools to drive our message. The problem is that of the starting point in the message, the message may be good but the delivery structure could well be polluted by past experiences and knowledge base, resulting in poor delivery and misunderstanding.

Organizations that implement a language design strategy must look at culture not on a national or regional level but on the level of the individual. To communicate to the majority effectively you must be understood by the individual. Mechanisms for allowing the individual to distance or phase out their own bias or prejudice short be encouraged. It is not only how we construct messages but also how we de construct and asses messages that can also lead to confusion and misunderstanding. There are many variables to the multi flow of globalised communications and Singlis and Brown (1995) explore a frame work that accounts for the influences that go towards understanding issues around multi cultural communications. Issues such as Self-construal,Independent self-construal. Cultural collectivism and self-construal, outcome variables, high-context communication, attributions to context and receiver and sender orientations all play a part in defining communication delivery and receiving of communications both at individual, organisational and global levels.

We can see that the art of communication is full of minefields and pit falls. Individuals should sit back and review communications with a more broad view and not attempt to over analyst. Setting clear boundaries about structure and content is of paramount importance. Being straight forward and avoiding cliches and humour will help especially in the written word. There have been many times on this course when I found myself reverting to humour to get my message across only on rereading did I censor myself because of the possibility of misunderstanding or in the case of my humour no understanding of the message I was trying to convey.

Social Capital – The foundation for success.

All organisations must embark on strategies that encourage exchanges and development of knowledge. Knowledge is the key to achieving competitive advantage in all levels of a firms operations. Within the parameters of international operations firms must work towards establishing mechanisms that encourage and facilitate communications at levels of cultural, social and technological understanding. Actively promoting the development of social capital is a a vital component of firms that function over wide geographic and cultural areas, because firms, even with large portfolios, have a common area the function of 'bonding' its employees can start at a simple and coercive level, that of the firms goals and objectives. Ownerships of corporate believes and philosophy is of paramount importance.

Any network, whether internal or external to the organisation should have in place or develop methods of relaying and reacting to information distribution. This is one area in which social capital can be developed for the benefit of corporate and partnership harmony.

The concept of Social Capital is now a key part of network development and communication. When organisations understand how each part interacts and individuals communicate with a clear overview of the firms positioning and objectives then learning and project fulfillment become easier. As Taylor (2007) says Social capital plays an essential role in nurturing the willingness and ability of employees to engage in the creation and sharing of knowledge in global firm. Establishing mechanisms that bond members of the organisation to each other and to the corporate view will pay benefits in better communications, innovation, problem solving and goal achievement. Getting the social structure right for the organisation is vital, socially communicative systems allow for individual relationship / understanding to develop within the organisation and increase the value and effectiveness of the firms human capital.

We can see, from our readings, that the concept of social capital has a very broad interpretation both internally and externally as illustrated by Adler and Kwon (2002). Depending on the perspective or interpretation we can use and flow the overview of the concept into practical operating programmes for firms to encourage and enhance operational efficiency.

At any level of organisational development social capital will play a role in moving the firm forward and placing it in a position of competitive advantage. Function of the organisation in local, global or glocal environments will need to employ mechanisms to enact social capital development internally and externally. The resulting improvement in communications will be seen in growth and deeper market penetration.

As a manager of a small community radio station and the chair of a national community media representative organisation I practice some form of social capital development every day. Community broadcasting plays an important part in developing social inclusion and participation within the communities it serves. While all community broadcasters operate within the same conceptual framework of beliefs and standards it is important the the 'oneness' of the movement is maintained. The practice of bringing together separate organisations within the 'belief network' is critical for the sustainability of the movement. Social capital practices are at the core of ensuring a stable direction and unity. The power of bringing people together under a common set of objectives ensures strength of commitment and message. This common bond development within any organisation or network is the foundation of growth as Van Vuuren (2001) says social capital requires a pro-active citizenry, that is, active and willing individuals with a sense of personal and collective capacities to produce desired outcomes.

No matter what size or operating area an organisation functions in, social capital is going to play a major part in its success or failure. Fail to grasp the concept of human interaction and learning within the organisation and there is the risk of fractures developing in the body of the organisation. Understand and accommodate the innate need for humans to communicate and the organisation, with careful management of delivery systems, will prosper.

Making the link between culture and organisation development. A case for crossvergence.

The approach of multi national organisations to integrating and harmonizing with the nations and cultures of their operating areas is open to various approaches. Instilling the organisations cultural approach can leave the firm with a situation that could foster segregation of product and culture. If the organisation has the resources and power to influence then it can impact on the target nations culture tendencies. We can see that large firms such as McDonalds and Coca Cola can influence cultural views and trends. This is most prevalent when looking at eating habits, the move towards fast food and it associated outcomes could be described as being able to change cultural eating traditions by removing the more collective eating traditions of some cultures. The question of how parent firms national and corporate culture impacts on target markets and subsidiary firms will play a major part in achieving competitive advantage.

The application of the various theories around convergence, divergence and crossvergence can influence the strategies of multi national firms in their penetration and establishment in new markets. Ralston (2008) definitions of the following show that influences on corporate make up and operations are a fine balance of bonding different aspects of cultural function and evolution.

Convergence can be seen as utalising the influence of technology to develop values and common understandings related to the use of technology, although one could see that these influences especially the power of media it should be seen very much on the basis of individuals interacting with knowledge and transferring that knowledge to others, forming the establishment of values sets and concepts.

Divergence is based on the believe that existing culture is strong and that individuals will maintain these values in the establishment and operation of the organisation. It could be seen as a system of maintaining and enriching cultural progress, however it does lead to a more inflexible global operation that may find itself in conflict with other areas of operation or markets.

Cross-vergence employs the resources and influences of both convergence and divergence theories resulting in a blending of influences that evolve a corporate and multinational standard of values and activities. By utilizing social cultural and technological principles organisations stand a better chance of integrating and competing in globalised markets.

In order to fully establish itself in a global economy organisation must embark in understanding and functioning within varied cultural and social markets while remaining in control and have understanding of situations as they emerge. Andrews and Chompusr (2001) state "we conclude that the conceptualization of 'crossvergent' managerial practices and values should be viewed less in terms of the culture divergence - convergence' dichotomy and more in terms of the working solutions to emerge at the 'corporate-societal' interface." If this is the case then the framework of cross-vergence development is a critical part of applying structure and communications within organisations emerging into the global market.

We must see globalision as a fusion of culture and not a mode of changing culture. crossvergence allow for the learning and teaching of different cultural perspective and allows for a functioning mechanism to be developed for organisations to compete in a changing global economy.

Games to play: Negotiating a meeting of minds.

Entering into negotiations between two culturally diverse organisations that operate in different social and political frameworks is a challenging task. We can see that the negotiations between Ericsson and the Chinese telecommunications organisations (CTO) described by Ghauri and Fang (2001) where long and strategic, almost a game of chess where one party knew the moves (Ericsson) and the other (CTO) new the strategy. Learning to negotiate with a strong counterpart requires meticulous planing and cultural understanding, although planning can only be achieved when information is available to act upon. In the case of Ericsson's negotiations with CTO a certain amount of on the job training was needed as situations and tactics presented themselves. Perceptions of purpose within the negotiating game can play a key role in achieving objectives. Ghauri and Fang (2001) listing of the Confucianism and Chinese stratagems help us understand the approach of Chinese negotiating tactics along with the understanding of the organisation – state relationship within China.

Approaching these negotiations requires the actioning of numerous cultural and management frameworks and theories to fully capitalize on negotiating situations. We can see that the key to successful conclusion is going to be the development of trust and strong personal relationships. Even within the collectivism of the Chinese teams the individual relationships will have a influencing impact of the outcome or at least the speed in which negotiations are carried out. Team structure and authority roles that differ within negotiating environments as occurred in the talks between Ericsson and CTO can be frustrating to the party with authority (Ericsson), especially when delays are part of the Chinese stratagem, however, from a CTO perspective this could well be a strong tool that effectively used would help achieve more concessions from Ericsson. Conflict between western rapid decision making corporate culture and the more apparent leisurely response times and need for repetitive explanations within the CTO structures can create a negative approach unless both parties can accommodate each others approaches to negotiations

Ensuring that structures are created that promote social capital and promote culturally efficient communications would be a paramount importance to facilitate successful on-going operations.

Applying mechanisms that counter or react to the tactics of the CTO Ericsson embarked on several applications of cultural understanding, in particular the importance to the Chinese delegation of saving face. The example of the Chinese delegate using incorrect information and how the correction was carried out by the Ericsson manager was a good example of understanding cultural perspective and enhancing individual relationships. The concept of not directly weakening or showing up an individual within a negotiating team allows for the formation of trust and the belief in the fact that negotiations are for the benefit of all parties. Ericsson's relationship development was instrumental in assisting the firm to reach a satisfactory conclusion. The development of informal relationships can assist firms capitalize on local practices and customs that allow corporate growth and smooth operational activities, however, western firms should be aware that in some situations these forms of relationships may be perceived as approaching corrupt as pointed out by Mead and Andrews (2009).

Ericsson's team were able to form connections with the methods of the CTO and enable their position to be incorporated into the conceptual structures required to function within the Chinese market. Understanding and adapting to the cultural characteristics of the CTO left Ericsson's team in a stronger position, even if behind the scenes the negotiating game was frustrating and protracted. Harmonizing with the collective culture and using it as a force of compliance was a strong tactical move on the part of Ericsson.

Concluding negotiations is only part of the process. Successful fulfillment and the potential for re-negotiating previously agreed points should be in the mind of negotiators when drawing up final agreements. There will be need for flexibility in cultures where the relationship between individuals is paramount, the written word needs to be taken in context with these relationship frameworks for true progress in the partnership to take place. The negotiating process described by Ghauri and Fang (2001) shows that with understanding, tolerance and a structured process of negotiating actions such as the three steps constructed by the authors of Pre-negotiation, Formal negotiation and post negotiation will enable firms to establish productive relationships that deliver in terms of meeting both parties objectives. Preparation is the key to entering the negotiating room. Being in possession of all the facts and being culturally sensitive is vital for the achievement of respect. Preparing the path must be the key as reinforced by Seng Woo and Prud'homme (1999) in negotiating with the Chinese, preparation is essential for successful negotiation.

Chapter 7

Strategic Operations Management

Introduction to strategic operations management Topics

Five basic principle for better operational understanding and efficiency.

Operating an organisation in an efficient manner is a requirement for competitive advantage. Understanding that the varied processes and actions of the firm and how those processes and actions interact and effect the outcome of the firm is a critical element of the operations manager. There is a need for operations managers to not only view the practical functions of deriving outputs through varied inputs but also accommodate the humanistic element of communication and interactions. Johnston (1999) stated 'We need to understand how all employees can deliver constant and consistent high levels of service and how we can design jobs and motivate employees to do this'. Operations Management should recognise the symbiotic and over lapping of the organisations activities used to deliver its goals and objectives. Performance within the firms operating environments is a fine balance of inputs resources and outputs.

When reviewing the operating processes of a firm the requirement to evaluate the effectiveness of the operations can be measured and understood through five performance objectives: quality, speed, dependability, flexibility and cost as described by Slack et al (2010). Each performance element will have an impact on each of the other elements and the operations manager must measure and balance activities to achieve a total output efficiency. To achieve competitive advantage the manager must work towards the 'idea' output for the firm, understanding the desired product or service required by customers and then fine tuning operations to reach optimum performance is the key to reaching sustainable and consistent output. It may well require the need to focus on key areas dependent on each product of service. When working towards a quality product that is delivered in a fixed and dependable manner then the elements of cost and flexibility become less significant in the family of performance elements.

The practical implementation of the five performance objectives when referring to my own organisation, a small 'not for profit' community radio station is as follows:

Quality – The need for consistent and listener focused output means that the firm must ensure programme output meets the needs of its customers and licensing requirements. Losing sight of customers and licensing authority quality would result in lost revenue and broadcasting rights. Therefore the need to maintain a quality output requires constant training and market evaluation resulting in higher costs. This is a priority for the station

Speed - Generally speed of delivery is not a driving factor for the station with the exception of news broadcasts with are delivered through external sources. However the news is not a key driver of the stations output and therefore could be seen as a low priority.

Dependability -Here there is a very strong internal and external dependability element. Internally we rely on the volunteers to deliver quality output at the appropriate time using the available resources of the the station. Externally listeners require a consistent output that meets their listening needs on a regular basis.

Flexibility - Variety of presenters means that the stations output and human resources must be flexible to accommodate changes in availability and situational output changes such as special event broadcasting outside of normal scheduling. This is a rare occurrence and there for plays a less prominent role in the day to day operations. However, the nature of funding requires that training and support services are highly flexible to utilize resources efficiently.

Costs - Being a not for profit organisation that is only allowed to derive a maximum of 50% of our revenue from commercial activities we are constantly looking at financial efficiency actions. The majority of costs are incurred through training, new and ongoing, and other volunteers support mechanisms. How costs are controlled and reduced is a high prominence in the station performance objectives.

Working through the five basic performance processes for a community radio station we can see that trade offs become necessary when financial resources are short, trade offs in flexibility will result in fewer outside broadcasts, trade off in quality results in fewer presenters and results in fewer new programmes and resulting reduction in quality of output. The role of the manager is to manipulate the processes of the firm in a manner that efficiently utilizes the resources available to maintain a customer view that promotes listenership loyalty and support levels to volunteers that enable continuous personal development. This repositioning of resources is an on going activity within community media management and by using the five basic principles mangers can better understand the consequences of repositioning functions and activities.

Operations strategy

Balanced strategies for competitive advantage.

Meeting the challenges of matching customer needs with available resources requires approaches from different disciplines within the organisation. Market requirement v's resource based strategy development should not be biased but complimentary Approaches to meeting these needs requires the managers to focus on operational activities and priorities to ensue a matching of key objectives. Identifying the competitive factors and other influencers will allow the allocation of available resources and highlight resource shortfalls. By focusing on competitive factors and their relationship to the organisations performance objectives the organisation can channel resources towards efficient delivery of its products or service. Performing to the delivery expectations of the external customers and meeting the internally set strategic objectives is a fine balance between external expectation and internal recourse allocation mechanisms. Developing resource based strategies helps meet customer needs through product design and efficient operational design that will help organisations reach competitive advantage. Grant (1991) concludes that ..'resource based approach to strategy formation is understanding the relationships between resources,capabilities, competitive advantage and profitability.'

Any market requirement based strategy needs to take into account the availability of resources and the organisations ability to facilitate the markets needs through the allocation of defined operational activity. If an organisation strifes to meet market or customer needs but is not prepared or able to achieve the levels required by customers in terms of it performance objectives then the firm is on a road to failure. Reaching a position where order winning factors are met in the eye of the customer must be built with resources and innovation Meeting the needs when there is a resource shortfall whether technological or financial requires understanding of organisational structure and capabilities as pointed out by Christensen and Bower (1996) By understanding the processes that link customer needs, impetus, and resource allocation, managers can align efforts to commercialize disruptive technology (which entails a change in strategy) with the forces of resource dependence.

In many 'start up' situations I have found myself with an identified product that meets the needs of its target audience. Developing the marketing strategy for the product will highlight shortfalls in resource availability. One of the major shortfalls has been a lack of substantial marketing budgets to get the product into the minds of the customer. Big press and local TV campaigns are out of the question so a radical re-think of how we reach our potential customers with available resources was needed. In a specific case I was starting a low cost airline in Spain with a limited amount of resources, constantly moving and refocusing operations to meet the needs of differing public, authority and internal needs. I wanted in the early days of establishing the airline to create a local and regional 'buzz' about the project. My solution was to convince the airport to allow us to establish our headquarters in the airport. We had a visible presence within the airport, lots of travelers and this led to lots of press interest, which we used very carefully, not to over expose but keep a drip drip of information flow. We had resources to establish offices and we used that to drive our early PR/promotions and investor relationship development.

Meeting the needs of customers is always going to be a challenge in the global marketplace, with rapidly changing expectations and desires customers become less fluid in product design and value. Utilizing an organisations resources correctly within its strategies is critical. Firms cannot develop strategies that can't be delivered because of resource shortfalls. It is only with a clear understanding of the tools a manger has around him/her that the strategy can be built and delivered. Organizations must meet the markets needs as illustrated by Slack et (2010) One of the key objectives for any organisation is to satisfy the requirements of its market. To achieve this I conclude that there should not be a clear differential in market or resource driven operational strategy but a hybrid that evolves the two approaches through innovation and flexibility.

Operational Structures

Globalization and the diversification of organisations across geographic areas and product portfolios means that traditional strategies need to be reviewed and adapted to meet globalised corporate structures needs. Kaplan and Norton (2006) noted that the traditional structures worked well but in the changing global environment new systems needed to be developed. The traditional product, geographic split can result in diverging strategy and objectives due to differing market and resource environments. Organizations centralising function processes and those decentralized by product and geographic make up needed to establish a more consolidated 'on message' approaches to distance segregated divisions strategic approaches. Kaplan and Norton (2006) propose that 'a management system based on the balanced scorecard framework is the best way to align strategy and structure.'

The need to balance approaches within operational and financial processes that allowed managers to access a fast accurate overview of the organisations position and functionality. By developing a balanced scorecard approach over four perspectives that Kaplan and Norton (2006) highlight means that the operations of the organisation can develop unity of purpose. How the balanced scorecard is derived within the business unit could be questioned as Boddy (2008) cites Akkermanns and Oorscot (2005) who ask whether it is the managers within the unit and their perspective produce the balanced scorecard. By setting the corporate structures and drivers from a central perspective within the core objectives of the firm managers can focus on deriving balanced scorecards that match the universal perspective of the firm.

Reviewing the four perspectives placed by Kaplan and Norton (2006) we can determine whether they will contribute to the establishment of a corporate unified evaluation perspective.

Financial Perspective.

Segregated business units operating under key financial indicators that match other business units under a corporate derived balance scorecard will give unified individual, geographic, product and corporate data to managers. This will give a better corporate governance structure, however, there maybe variances within the data because of business unit uniqueness. Measuring systems and analysis should account for variable data flows and assessment bias within units.

Customer Perspective.

Developing cross organisation customer interactions by understanding need and offering economies in dealing across the corporation. Cross selling while maintaining customer satisfaction demands will lead to greater corporation output. Measuring customer satisfaction on agreed level of understanding allows managers to evaluate and compare business unit performance.

Process Perspective.

Units operating similar processes can unite to take advantage of savings made by sharing resources. Technological exploitation across the organisations activities can offer competitive advantage through delivering across the organisations markets and with it customers. When processes are centralized the organisations individual business units can risk damage through performance short comings in other process controlling units. Managers must, even when using centralized processes, keep their eye on the ball within the functionality of their units.

Learning and Growth Perspective.

Standardising approaches to continuous personal development and the utalisation of activities around human capital development will allow the firm to establish mechanisms to maximise innovation and knowledge development. Ensuring that knowledge is transferable requires the implementing of best   practice models to instigate better communications internally and externally. Balanced scorecard measurement also for more accurate and accountable   analysis

Aligning operational structures and processes across globalised organisations is a critical strategic objective. Being able to view the entire organizations performance against known factors that interchange with the organisation business units will allow specific comparisons and assessments Kaplan and Norton (2006) proposals suggest that the balanced scorecard approach can facilitate better understanding with organisations and allow the establishment of strategies that unite and act individually within the organisation. However, how those balanced scorecards are derived as been questioned and I would suggest that the establishment of strategic objectives in individual business units based on the corporate scorecard models would need to be monitored independently to ensure that mangers perspective did not distort data and interpretation. The variations in operating realities as been recognized by Kaplan and Norton (2006) who acknowledge the difficulties in establishing balanced scorecards that reflect business unit uniqueness and the corporate overview. Even so I believe the evolutionary nature of the globalised organisation will account and adapt systems and methods that allow mechanisms that enable managers to get a better,truer view and interpretation of the organisations performance at all levels of operations. We need to use tools and mechanisms such as those proposed by Kaplan and Norton (2006) but, like the traditional methods of product and geographic diversified structures have become superseded, so the balanced scorecard system will evolve and other factors introduced to enhance strategic development within resource availability and operational processes.

Operations design

Best_Practice

Whether a firm wishes to redesign its operations or not the need to remain competitive will always dictate that operations achieve the most efficient and effective delivery mechanisms. Redesigning processes by managers needs to be assessed with the unique perspective of the organisation. Broad frameworks of redesign can help managers focus on issues but will require the need to fine tune and harmonize into the organisations existing structure and culture. There could be an argument to approach redesign from the point of a clean sheet as described by   Reijers and Mansar (2004), however, there can be risks associated with this approach. Greater challenges around creating cultural, practical function and human resource miscalculation and misunderstanding. We will explore frameworks that operate within existing functionality of the firm. Working with what we have allows for more resource focused redesigning of process mechanisms.

Streamlining inter-company processes isn't just an interesting idea; it's the next frontier of efficiency. Hammer (2001). Redesigning for efficiency and maintaining competitive advantage is a process that mangers must face on a regular basis. Redesigning the mechanisms of the firms processes does not need to be major restructuring but can be a simple process of identifying fractional moves to deliver efficiency improvements.

Working on the frameworks identified by Reijers and Mansar (2004) will assist the manger embark on the road of redesigning organisational process mechanisms suitable for their environment do operations. These generic approaches to redesign should be explored by managers with the view from the point of the technical challenges and the socio-cultural challenges. There will be other challenges for managers but as with all generic approaches they must be evolved and tuned to the functionality of the firm. Reijers and Mansar (2004) highlight Alters framework which suggests that a work-centered analysis framework that is consistent with the CIMOSA enterprise model view, in that it takes the view that the following areas should be considered: Function view, Information view, resource view and organisational view. Although Alter appears to have close associations with CIMOSA the six areas of linked process with the use of technological development would fit the modern firms BPR objectives. On the basis that organisations are evolving into symbiotic entities that function through linked action and reaction.

I have always found that managing firms involves continuous redesign of processes to accommodate changes in the market and available resources. The redesign activities never seem to be strategic but more reactive to environmental changes. There are going to be times when firms require wholesale operational redesign because of poor management and a lack of a clear over view of the firms actions and position in the market. Redesign should be a evolutionary process and not a revolution unless all systems and processes have broken and ceased to function. Adopting the correct generic framework will be vital for the successful redesigning of failed or failing organisations, however, I believe that ongoing enhancement, refocusing and fine tuning of processes that accounts for the cross linked process effects is the best way to proceed. Understanding and predicting the 'knock on' effect of changes and analyzing the output results down the process chain is the key to successful customized business process redesign.

BPR frameworks are there to guide and not dictate to managers when embarking on redesign actions. Generic approaches result in generic answers and do not lead to true innovation when redesigning process. Organizations are functioning organisms that respond and react to their environment and need to be treated in a manner that accommodates their sensitivities to their internal and external audiences. Understand the organisation and redesign is a painless and profitable action. Misunderstand the organisation and there will be pain and loss. Best practice is to focus on the organisation and its unique situation. Paper and Chang (2005) illustrate the need for organisation based custom redesign processes 'A BPR methodology is not a 'turn-key' program and should not be purchased as such. Each organization has its own special needs, environment, and business culture.'

Operations organisation

Smart network development and entry.

The changing operating boundaries and mechanisms within the globalised market are pushing the way in which business structures, organisations and individuals interact and communicate to achieve more effective and profitable outcomes for the firm. The relationships and partnerships developed to meet global market demands through the web and other internet and communication modes has allowed organisations reach greater and more diverse markets. However, this increase in market and changing communication systems has required managers to review and change ways in which they act with customers and partners in the operations to reach these new customers.

To meet the changing environment and maintain competitive advantage firms are required to develop functional and mutual partnerships that operate in a multi linked and organic manner in order to respond to market and production changes. These interactions have been described as being smart interactions that respond and react in a given manner that acts or mimics biological actions. A collection of inputs or swarms behave in predictable ways that allow firms to function collectively for mutual benefit.

The concept of swarm like actions operating in a smart fashion created by firms forming links and partnerships through technology is playing a greater role. The examples of Amazon and Ebay highlighted by van Heck & Vervest (2007) are good illustrators of the swarm approach of transacting business in a global market. The application of technological systems to moderate and facilitate operational processes becomes a critical element in providing links and markets for diverse sellers and customers. This fast moving network system has resulted in more firms moving from the slower traditional forms of business delivery operations.

With the move to more networked business development one could ask the question as to whether it is still beneficial for smaller firms to move towards integration as larger players can execute interactions faster and more effectively through greater resource availability. The situation earlier in network development meant that the smaller organisation was able to take full advantage of the emerging systems because they were more flexible and innovative. Today in a proven market entry is more complex and competitive.

Heck & Vervest (2007) proposal that firms should move towards a new business network system over the more traditional value chain system would be a risky strategy due to the advancing state of the global market. Positioning within a global network is becoming more complex and resource intense. Establishing a traditional business in a global network will require the application of new delivery mechanisms in terms of marketing and logistics. However, the smaller firm seems to be in a stronger position once established as pointed out by Kauffman & Wang (2008) Large firm size, we found, was also associated with a higher likelihood of bankruptcy or liquidation among Internet firms.

Incorporating networked business operating systems in a traditional sense would allow for the delivery of more established customer value models to be part of the networked service towards customer retention. The focus on business network operations systems is an evolving and managers must be flexible and innovative to meet market and customer changes. Goldman et al (2009) state that 'After little more than a decade, it is once again necessary to rethink organizational structures in order to support dynamic collaboration across ever more porous enterprise boundaries.'

Working smarter and more integrated within target markets on a global scale is a solid strategy for the modern firm, even with concerns around market entry resource issues for smaller organisations, providing the managers develop strategies focused on the new network structure and does not directly translate traditional value chains into the new technological based network systems. Maintaining human value ethics within the new structures will be a key to success. The de-humanizing of communication mechanisms within customer contact should be avoided and mechanisms must be in place to value the customer. Efficiency within the network will only be effective when successful output is sustainable over time and through change.

To conclude it is important to recognize that the proposition that new network systems based on technological links and interactions may offer advantages and larger markets to the firm it is not a 'fix it all' mechanism for organisations. There is still a strong need to establish strong functional strategies that fit with the new network operating framework and do not just migrate traditional operating strategies to new systems. Strong reactive and innovative strategies are required to succeed as pointed out by Vervest (2006)

Companies must develop and act "smart" in rapidly changing and expanding business networks enabled by today's pervasive communications technologies.

Operations Technology

Global Integration

Changes to how organisations structure themselves within a global market is going to be a major challenge. Developments in technology, communications and global markets mean that firms must review and analyst the very nature of their own existence. The organisations evolution over the past 150 years or so has been gradual and adaptive to the innovations of its time. Even though these changes were reactive to political and geographical changes they were influenced by technology movement, however, there was still a traditional form even when firms moved from national to multinational structures. Today we see global organizations linking and integrating functions across boundaries for competitive advantage. This integration is currently based on the extension of the traditional multinational corporation structures. New ways of interacting and trading along with new functioning standards will develop over coming years and we should challenge our existing structure and foster new 'out of the box' formats and mechanisms. This need to approach future structure to capitalize on true global integration was addressed by Palmisano (2006) the premium comes from the fusion of invention and insight into how to transform how things are done.

The organic structure of the modern organisation will allow leaps of faith when it comes to evolving structure but maybe we need to start again with a blank sheet and form new organisation formats and structures better able to function in the new and rapidly changing markets. Childs (2005) describes the traditional organisation as structural, processual and boundary defining facets.These characteristics have until now stood the test of time but now the regimented approaches may need to be re-evaluated to fully integrate firms activities within a global context. Movements in technology and communications have shown that the firm can more readily outsource and import activities and processes that are not restricted by geographic boundaries.

The use of technology in all its forms will play a significant role in forming a new global organisation order, but the key to true change will not be in the hardware and software of the technology but in the way we culturally and socially bond to build a global village that exists in a dynamic and cooperative manner that benefits all its citizens. This approach is not without support Higgins-Desbiolles (2006) fairer and sustainable systems could be developed to displace the divisive and destructive dynamics of capitalist globalization

New applications 'in the making' with current global situations and technological availability can be seen evolving, especially within marketing and sales structures. Online activities can be seen as key drivers within sole traders and major organisations. This development that allows international trade will help evolve organisational forms, whether those forms are evolutionary or revolutionary will depend on how 'free' managers feel in developing the environment around them. Greater flexibility in network development and supply chains will open up many opportunities for firms providing the network flows are consistent and sustainable. More diverse supply networks will require strong partnership relationships based on new organisational structural systems capitalizing on technological advances and cultural and social understanding.

The future may be bright and global integration possible but only if we can come to terms with cultural and social diversity along with technological exploitation. To make predictions for future integrated structures is best summed up by Jarvenpaa and Ives (1994) who concluded.... we fear that all of our experiences in the present and past limit our ability to conceive the future.

Planning and control

Demand Management

Demand Management is a vital part of an organisations success. The planning and control of operational activities is the key to meeting the needs of customers in a manner that facilitates loyalty and consistency. Being in a position of knowing or accurately predicting demand from customers leaves managers with the ability to adopt the most efficient mechanisms for delivery. By identifying potential variances and seasonal fluctuations production activity can be fine tuned to operate at it optimum level for the output required. Adjusting and even reallocating resources becomes more practicable and allows for less wastage in terms of innovatory and human resources. Adapting the operations process to meet demand will assist in the generation of higher customer / user satisfaction due to fewer delivery failures. Producing enough to meet demand and have contingencies for production failures or logistics complications is also a vital part of the planning and control process.

Theoretical and practicable approaches to demand management to ensure all round satisfaction to customers and suppliers requires a flow of data in order to facilitate efficient operational flows. This need to accommodate all areas of contact to ensure satisfaction is pointed out by Heikkilä (2002) Demand chain management understands the need for good customer–supplier relationships and reliable information flows as contributors to high efficiency.

Demand management, in the planning and control of the activities to delivery product or service to the customer in the most profitable and efficient manner requires understanding of the demand needs, managers must look at the consistency or fluctuations of demand in order to plan activities and accommodate effective delivery while being able to quickly adjust activities to meet unforeseen variations in demand, either positive or negative.

Recognizing demand ratios and ensuring that the organisation is capable of meeting the capacity requirements need to ensure delivery is paramount for the management of the organisation. By defining the various models of demand the manager can plan operational activity and ensure that the most efficient form of action is maintained. When looking at the different demand and capacity models as described by Slack et al (2010) we can better understand required actions.

Variable demand is going to facilitate the least efficient and effective use of capacity functions. Dependent demand is going to offer stable delivery criteria as it is the most predictable of the demand flow.

Independent demand is the most unpredictable model with customer driven flexible requirements, uncertainty in customer trends due to changes in public exposure to the product in either a favorable or negative manner. One example would have been the television broadcast highlighting the favorable effects of a low cost wrinkle cream produced by Boots Pharmacies in the UK. All supplies where sold the following day and future supplies were restricted until the firm could adjust it production activities. Talking about the event Mr Baker, chief executive of Alliance Boots, said: "We're absolutely delighted. It's taken us about three weeks to get the product back into supply" (BBC, 2007)

Strategies for dealing with demand variances can be categorized in to two key areas of production mechanisms:

Level – This involves a continuous flow of production that does not account for the fluctuations in demand. It relies on maintaining stock levels to meet increased demand, however, the high innovatory costs can significantly impact on profitability.

Chase – This requires the adjustment of production activity to match as closely as possible the direct demand. While this offers a more efficient means in terms of lower innovatory it does open the firm to risks if fluctuations in demand outstrip capacity as there are no reserves.

Taking the example of the online delivery of educational products by a university we can see how best to meet the needs of the customer/student while utalising the most efficient use of the universities resources, lecturers, support staff and technology. The key area of demand is going to be the interaction of the lecturer and student. Meeting the demand of the student is key as Volery and Lord (2000) says the level of interaction between the students and the lecturer appears predominant in online delivery.

Online Universities need to fully utilize technology in order to deliver effectively, however the need to ensure that staff are well versed in communicating via online activities is critical. Once the university as ensured is delivery mechanisms and protocols are functional they would need to ensure a constant flow of students. Traditionally students would start study programmes at single fixed point in the year. By offering multi start points throughout the year universities can meet customer flexibility demand and account for and replace fallout throughout the year. Of course demand for courses are going to be unpredictable and would be influenced by various external factors and traditional learning trends. At best one could assume that the demand cycle for education is customer driven without too much predicability and therefore could categories demand as Independent. Universities can meet this through flexible human resource allocation and technology deployment.

Demand Management will play a growing role in ensuring organisation compete competitively and are able to satisfy customer needs. This is even more essential for firms in a global fast moving and highly flexible market. This is supported by Gupta & Kohli (2006) when talking about Enterprise Resource Planning (ERP) The global competition, along with shorter product life-cycles, ever-increasing market niches, and the pressure to react quickly to the changing external business environment has forced companies to make decisions in an integrated manner. How we plan and control the firms activities and relationships with customer demand and expectations is critical to successful strategic delivery.

Identifying a strategy for improvement

Performance Measurement

The ability to access and retrieve information is the cornerstone of academic development. Being able to focus on a single, or at least fewer sources of information, is a tremendous benefit to the student. A wide range of information that is easily accessible through fast technology and accurate cataloging play a significant role in ensuring a library is seen as 'worth while' by its customers. Delivering data into the hands of student and academics is the driving factor in a university library and its customers should be seen as driving factor in the operational development and performance assessment.

Libraries should not see themselves as collectors of knowledge but distributers. It is the management of a libraries performance in delivering to it core customer base that will ensure excellence. How libraries have evolved to meet the modern challenges of need with technology has changed the face and operations of the institutions. One such change is the has been the ability to rent data electronically, removing the need to collect and store hard copy. Ross & Sennyey (2008) state that "Since digital collections are seldom bought, but rather rented, the concept of building collections becomes anachronistic. A digital library assembles a series of rental contracts that meet current patron needs, renewed or cancelled according to negotiable terms."

Approaches to the performance management of modern library operations would still require the meeting of customer expectation from the perspective of library and strive to achieve a level of output that aims to reach or exceed the perceptions of the customer. Assessing performance through the five objective indicators (cost, speed, quality, flexibility, and dependability) can help in ensuring that the internal operations are tuned to meet the needs of the external audience. The current mechanisms deployed by libraries to maximise data availability is also dependent on external organisations operational performance. Using rental contracts to achieve and manage the increasing amount of research and other papers that are being made available and demanded by consumers will require continuous monitoring and evaluation to ensure quality of output. Employing approaches that meet this need, such as Total quality management (TQM) systems will form a strong element in ensuring that the needs and expectations of the customer are met. It has been shown that applying TQM systems into academic libraries it will show a positive impact on customer needs Wang (2006) concludes "Studies of both theoretical principles and experimental implementations demonstrate that it is worthwhile to introduce TQM to the academic libraries."

Accessing information that is 'fit for purpose 'is a vital part of any libraries function and ensuring that this requirement is met then continuos evaluation of available data is required. Operationally the library must deliver on information availability and mechanisms that deliver that information to the customer. The use of external electronic publications allows for a greater range of data with a reduced cost implication because of the rental aspect. Acquiring information only when it is required can have significant impact on costs in that there is no need to purchase outright and the savings in cataloging and storing due to the work being carried out externally. Libraries need to ensure that their technical skill base meets the needs of the delivery mechanisms.

The effective performance of a library would be viewed in terms of its quality output and as such institutions should strive to meet the growing needs of the customer in a rapidly changing and accessible knowledge based world. Sahu (2007) states that Quality cannot be provided solely by focusing on systems and procedures; it must also be focused on the client/user. While systems and procedures are strong elements of the performance criteria they should not over power the customer need by disenfranchising them from accessibility. Ensuring that availability of data that is fit for purpose is also a vital part of performance assessment along with the systems and technology that are at the front line of delivery.

Preventing failure and securing quality

TQM'v'SS

Achieving the highest levels of quality and correspondent efficiency requires mechanisms to evaluate and adapt actions in order to reach full potential both internally and externally. Total Quality Management (TQM) and Six Sigma are systems that allow managers to explore and reduce the levels of poor quality and thus reduce waste. The continuous monitoring of the organisations activities in order to refine and improve activities using either TQM or Six Sigma requires a complete 'buy in' by all members of the organisation. The use of these to systems fit well into manufacturing environments and have also been utilized within the service sector with some modification that provides a SERVQUAL model as highlighted by Boddy (2008). Each system requires continuos improvement and refining of activities, the concept that 'there is always room for improvement' holds well with both TQM and Six Sigma.

As Slack et al (2010) point out even when labels are not used the fundamentals of TQM have entered the organisational environment. Quality improvement is now an everyday function of successful firms no matter how they carryout the function or which mechanisms they employ.

TQM – the general belief that by not having perfect quality leads to a waste in recourses. These resources include lost, unused or scraped materials. Lost and wasted time along with poor communication and lack of understanding within the processes.

Six Sigma – A statistical/data driven approach to identify defective processes and activities throughout the organisation.

Which ever quality evaluation model a firm uses, or even combination, it is an activity that should be followed through practically and not just given lip service within the entire organisational network. For a successful outcome management and employees must embrace the process and its outcomes.

Chester Royal Hospital, UK were having issues regarding late and lost patient notes. These notes were note being made available to doctors on time to see patients leading to poor customer service and back logs of patients. Note were meant to be held by a central records dept. and delivered to doctors by an internal mail system. Management embarked on a review of this specific process and mechanisms using TQM. They identified specific quality issues around the 'ownership' of records and the tracking records maintained at the central office. Several recommendations were made including enforcing the record tracking system, improved personnel identification of doctors assistant for mail deceivers and rescheduled delivery times to meet the appointment rotas. The implementation of these new guidelines rapidly reduced the amount of lost files and assisted in improving patient throughput. Broddy (2008) does however highlight that there was some resistance because staff felt they were 'losing authority over the records'

One of the big issues around improvement is the aspect of implementing change and as we can see with the Chester Royal Hospital resistance can be an issue that must be accounted for when implementing change for improvement. The importance of staff buy in cannot be over emphasized when firm undergo changes.

Ford Motor Company moved to six sigma in 1999, a migration from TQM. According to Coronado and Antony (2002) Fords use of TQM was driven by fixing faults no matter the cost, with the introduction of six sigma engineers carried out cost benefit analysis to ascertain its value. The expected process performance improvement i.e. reduction of rework, scrap rate, reduction of warranty costs, reduction of process variability, etc.) is about 70 per cent per project. They go on to state that Ford see six sigma as a more profit driven system than their previous TQM activities.

Which ever system a company employs to improve its quality and performance will to some extent depend on the culture of the firm. While six sigma may offer a more profit driven result TQM as been instrumental in developing the concept of controlling waste. A philosophy that may well find itself re-emerging in larger organisations as we strife to be more environmentally aware and responsible.

Before engaging any of the systems described mangers should carryout extensive awareness training with staff to ensure that there is understanding and acceptance of the activities and their consequences. Coronado and Antony (2002) A communication plan is important in order to involve the personnel with the six sigma initiative by showing them how it works, how it is related to their jobs and the benefits from it.

Mangers may see TQM as a more strategic approach and Six Sigma as a more operational approach. Either way each can play its part when applied in the right area and right manner to improve the total range of activities within the organisation.

Chapter 8

Organisational Learning

Knowledge is a valuable currency in a global market, but knowledge in an organisation is useless unless it is understood and used in a strategic manner to channel the firm towards a position of competitive advantage. The use and management of knowledge is a growing driver in the development of today's organisation and the systems utilized to ensure the collecting and efficient use data is becoming more technologically dependent. Strategic development is reliant on having and understanding key market data and being able to flexibly alter strategic objectives when this data indicates a need.

Knowledge becomes redundant when it is misplaced or not understood. Dierkes et al (2003) Ch11 example of Xerox' failure to understand new technological implications is an example of this. The interpretation of information by managers can be a subjective activity and the implementation of that interpretation can result in negative outcomes, therefore, organisations should not rely on individuals to solely analyze key data or choose which pieces of data are used. Learning within the organisation is a collective act that should also acknowledge the role of the individual.

Organizations are evolving bodies that, like their operators collect and utilize internal and external knowledge to adapt and achieve higher levels of survival and success. The organisational process of managing this knowledge is widely researched and seen as a critical element of organisational survival. To fully capitalize on the knowledge currency firms must be proactive in the collection and distribution of all aspects of knowledge. The developing of learning and distribution systems plays a vital role in the smooth transfer of knowledge up and down the corporate stream.

Historically learning has been about training within the workplace, however, this has not always been successful in terms of real transfer and implementation of knowledge. Laiken, (2001) states "Despite highly successful experiences within a classroom setting, specific outcomes have been difficult to assess, and links between such non- formal learning opportunities and their actual impact on the job almost impossible to ascertain with any confidence" The concept of learning within work practice and process shows a more beneficial outcome for the organisation. Laiken (2001) went on to conclude that learning should be a balance between organisational and individual learning. Alavi and Leidner (2001) define the role of the individual within the organizations learning processes as 'knowledge is not so much a capability for specific action, but the capacity to use information; learning and experience result in an ability to interpret information and to ascertain what information is necessary in decision making.'

The concept of learning for the organisation and the individual is part of the policy of the Community Radio Forum of Ireland a body that supports and promotes community media in Ireland. With 20 licensed radio stations and 40 aspiring stations they needed to share experiences and knowledge for the benefit of all members. To do this they developed a knowledge sharing system based on a principle of mutual cooperation and knowledge pooling "learning through shared experiences". Through their website www.craol.ie stations can have access to documents including policy statements, successful funding applications, programmes, technical information, research, training materials and individual experiences. The addition of all this information as helped boost the operations and quality of community radio in Ireland. The sharing of knowledge is a key driver in developing community radio across the country.

Knowledge plays a vital role in the establishment of competitive advantage for an organisation. That learning process should be focused on organisational and individual systems to achieve true growth. Learning should be an on going process that is part of the everyday activities of the firm and not exclusively focused on knowledge transfer through the classroom. Learning is an organic process within the development of the individual and organisation and managers should value and encourage proactively participate in collecting and sharing experiences. For the organisation the objective of learning is the continued growth and success of all its activities and processes.

Performance through learning – knowledge for growth.

Achieving competitive advantage in a global environment entails mechanisms that adapt and advance products and services in line with customer needs or perceptions. The concept of the learning organisation as being the most successful would stand well in the world of evolutionary organic growth of a firm. To learn from numerous data inputs and maintain the corporate knowledge base is a key component of today's international organisation. The learning organisation can of come in to being when the collection of knowledge by the individual is transferable as Gomez et al (2005) states the knowledge acquired and created on an individual level has to be transferred and integrated into the organization. To fully accept the influence of organisational learning on a firms performance we must look at the mechanisms to distribute and embed knowledge within the firm. Measuring the learning impact requires a statistical and observational approach that accounts for cultural and social learning defaults. The measurement of business performance against evidence of organisational learning trends and activities will help establish patterns of behavior for managers to maintain or establish competitive advantage through organisational learning.

Analysis of Lopez et al 3 hypotheses.

The 3 hypotheses proposed by Lopez et al (2005) would on the surface seem to hold true based on general observations from managers. It is the learning mechanisms adopted by organisations that would determine how successful knowledge acquisition is translated into competitive advantage and financially lucrative activities.

If organisational learning is a key component of the sustainable firm then we would be able to see patterns of learning emerge from studies. Lopez et al (2005) methodology of using Spanish firms may well reflect the position in Spain, however, social and corporate culture will also impact on the efficiency and predisposition to learning mechanisms. The collection of explicit data, even in the recognized 'multidimensional character of learning', is going to be influenced by the characteristics of cultural and social conditioning towards learning and therefore biased towards the cultural learning default.

In order to support their hypotheses Lopez et al (2005) use a rigid data interpretation methodology that relies on statistical rather than observational data. This approach may well offer a more confirmatory approach as they highlight but the data is flawed because of the potential idealistic approach of the contributors to the survey. Managers believe that they are implementing the perfect processes while the reality may be different. This lack of observational data may skew the true image of the benefits of organisational learning outputs.

One of the areas explored within the paper was the relationship between internal and externally acquired knowledge and the proposal that these to factors integrate within the organisation. The conclusion that this is the case would stand to reason when developing innovative products or processes because customer satisfaction is achieved by meeting needs from available / acquirable resources and/or known customer need.

It would seem that the organisational learning inputs and knowledge transfer related well to the hypotheses of the team and that the statistical interpretation of data collected supports such concepts. It would be wise to question the strict validity of purely statistical data that may have been delivered in a biased manner without observational data to support its validity. Measuring learning in the format described by the authors is only one tool in the interpretation of the effects of organisational leaning systems and outputs. Of course, from the data analyses we can see the correlation between learning and success but this only goes part of the way in delivering a greater picture of the learning influence in a modern organisation. Successful learning techniques today may result in a stagnation in future development unless learning is perceived as changeable in order to fit the social and cultural learning default of the firm and its operating nation.

While Lopez et al confirm the perceived view that organisational learning positively influences the competitive advantage of the firm it does offer only a narrow perspective on the subject. It would be interesting to view the data if it was collected across a range of geographical, social and cultural backgrounds. In today's technologic society the concept of learning and developing are engrained in our corporate cultures. Companies must listen to the needs of customers and pay attention to knowledge development within their own organisation. Failure to engage in knowledge transference and development can result in serious loss, however, pay attention and the benefits can be very rewarding as Microsoft and Apple discovered through the use of discarded Xerox technology.

Collective Knowledge

The heart of any organisation is the collective knowledge it processes in order to deliver on its strategic goals. The use of this knowledge and the mechanisms to facilitate knowledge creation and distribution are the life force of the firm. In many organisation this movement of knowledge is little understood and even accepted as an evolutionary element of organisational development. Better understanding of the mechanisms will facilitate 'better' learning and sharing of experiences within the company.

Today we see the need to stay ahead of the competition and maintain competitive advantage through the exploitation of technology and the use of rapid communication systems. These systems can encourage the sharing of explicit knowledge and encourage the recognition of the importance of tacit knowledge and its need to be made explicit for continued organisational advancement. The ease and familiarity of these systems can increase the sharing of both tacit and explicit knowledge as described by Wasko & Faraj, (2000) cited by Hall (2001) 'The broad theme of "ease of use" can be extended to argue that tools for knowledge sharing should be integrated into communities to match the levels of formality operated in the work groups that they serve' Creating Knowledge, communicating knowledge and acting on knowledge will drive a firm forward and strengthen its core elements.

Knowledge creation process can be divided into 3 layers as described in Dierkes et al (2003) SECI, Ba and knowledge assets.Comprehending the path taken by the knowledge chain will allow managers to integrate interactive mechanisms for the sharing, creating and distributing knowledge. Socialization-externalization- combination and internalization process theory (SECI) describes the ways in which knowledge is converted within the organisation.

Creating an environment that facilitates the open movement of knowledge is described by Dierkes et al (2003) as a need to establish a feeling within the organisation of 'Love, Care, Trust and Commitment'. Harmonious and non competitive relationships are paramount to forming learning areas described as 'Ba' This concept of an area for exchange may or may not take on the physical facility by a technological area or cyber space, it could even manifest itself in external social activities. Managers should work towards enacting activities and actions that create 'safe sharing zones' do Ba.

Although we see knowledge as tacit or explicit the knowledge assets are categorized by Nonaka, Toyama and Konno (2000) into 4 areas: Experiential, Conceptual, Systemic and Routine knowledge assets. By mapping these process we can re start the process of knowledge creation and sharing using SECI for the development of a continuous organisational culture of learning.

Knowledge creates value within an organisation by facilitating growth and efficiency across the entire network of the firm. Continuos personal and corporate professional development enhances all aspects of company internally and externally. Using the principles of the SECI, Ba and knowledge asset the organization I chair carries out regular 'training through sharing' events over a year. Broadcasters, Managers and board members come together to gain and share experiences about community media. Sharing of learnt experience in a formal way through workshops and lectures plays an important role in developing the community media network in Ireland. Lessons learnt at these events are then transported to stations and relaid to other volunteers and staff. One of the aspects of these events is that when we ask attendees for feedback they say that they gained the most knowledge from the social activities in the bar. The bar here can be seen as to represent the 'Ba' environment described by Dierkes et al (2003). It is a safe area for open non competitive sharing of information.

The learning mechanisms found in organisations could be seen as a natural development of the collective behavior of humans. It is by exploring these mechanisms that managers can foster environments and systems that encourage exchange of knowledge and its development into corporately beneficial actions. By capitalizing on the human thirst for knowledge managers who understand the process can facilitate a more harmonious and productive organisation. Learning is not a science it is an experience that can be described by science.

Knowledge creation and its future path.

Knowledge possessed by the individual within the organisation is a valuable asset. The task of integrating that knowledge into the firms knowledge assets and using given tacit and explicit knowledge as a source of knowledge creation is a key driver for a sustainable organisation. Nonaka et al (2006) exploration of knowledge creation theory highlights the evolutionary development of the theory and its integration into todays knowledge driven firms. This work gives a view that the theory is being practiced in some part by organisations and while there is an element of practicality linked to this the implementation is not so practical for most firms.

The premise that organisations are actively engaging structures that promote knowledge creation is unconvincing on the basis that most mangers do not understand the mechanisms and psychology of the individuals instinct to protect knowledge for self preservation in competitive environments. To help facilitate the trust and confidence to encourage imparting and promotion of knowledge requires the correct psychological environment as pointed out by McAdam et al (2007) organizations should focus on creating a "knowledge culture" that encourages learning and the creation and sharing of knowledge. This fragile and historically founded knowledge possessed by members of the firm is recognized in the paper and is separated from the concept of information relaying around the company.

Knowledge Creation over information

While outlining the basics of SECI and its role in the organisation the paper also identifies the weaknesses of maintaining mechanisms to foster knowledge creation and it onward path in the firm. Most organisations would find implementation of SECI difficult to implement when diverse and speculative variations in theories are abound, however, the use of the theory and its growing use in organisations structures and practices means that the evolutionary integration and practices will play a more dominant part in the development of smaller and more established structures and firms.

The establishment of the devision between knowledge and information seems a helpful step to understanding the role of the theory in a practical setting along with the clear outline of the processes of knowledge creation such as vision,activism, organisational form and leadership. All of this helps the firm move towards the concept of a knowledge strategy according to Nonaka et al (2006). If this is the case then we will see the processes more prominent in future organisational development strategies. As the paper points out the key to true knowledge creation is the establishment of ba within the whole knowledge process and as highlighted earlier in this paper will help foster the trust and openness needed to exchange tacit and explicit knowledge. Without ba the authors rightly state that knowledge separated from the free flow exchange of ba becomes information and is available just for transmission. While there is some concern regarding the role of ba in creativity, the paper highlights two key areas including the fostering of group thinking rather than a free spirit approach, with careful control and facilitation that challenges concepts ba can offer safe zone of discovery. The use of activism and vision will inspire the process and strengthen creativity according to Nonaka et al (2006). If this is the case it will only work if the activists can facilitate in a non biased way and resist planting concepts or collective views.

The role of organisation structure is also explored and shows that hierarchical and bureaucratical forms properly fail in effective knowledge creation, an understandable view in that such a structure relies in passing instruction and information and does not foster free thinking. According to the Nonaka et al (2006) efficient knowledge creation would seem to work in flatter organisations where leadership was more enabling rather than controlling and directing. This would seem to fit with the general nature of learning and sharing environments and firms should establish mechanisms to flatten learning exchange systems even if a more hierarchical and bureaucratical form is the structure of the firm. To fully capture the potential of knowledge creation firms need not undertake complete organisation restructuring.

Practical knowledge creation

Japanese mobile firm utilized knowledge creation theory to develop i-mode, a mobile internet technology. The implementation of SECI and ba played a vital role when 3 managers with extensive tacit knowledge where brought together by the firm to develop i-mode. In their study of the firms processes Peltokorpi et al (2007) state The innovation of i-mode was largely based on leading and organizing ba and on their interactions.

It is not the case that organisations must instigate organisation wide knowledge creation but they can target specific strategic or innovative targets by creating knowledge creating teams. This will assist the evolutionary process of making knowledge creation part of the organisation culture.

The paper compressively reviews the situation within organisations with regard to knowledge creation and draws on various strands of evidence and research. It gives an understandable perspective on the current standing of knowledge theory and it route to its current position. One can see that the whole development of the theory and in practice is going to be a very evolutionary road that will evolve to meet the organisational environments it is implemented. Research should follow the evolutionary path and evaluate best practice and implementation mechanisms.

Work Systems

The operating of work systems should be a continuos process of input and output improvements. Managers should allow themselves to evaluate the functionality and efficiency of existing systems and strive to improve at all levels. Organisational learning within the more traditional company structure, especially the more rigid approaches of economic theory including the neoclassics, mean that new and relatively undefined theories of organisational learning find it difficult to penetrate the organisational collective or culture.

One could argue that the application of Bayesian learning allows economists to integrate learning processes into their activities, however as Dierkes et al (2007) point out this is not the necessarily the case when elements of human psychology are included and it may be that Bayesian approaches are too costly when a humans natural instincts respond to markets rather than the intellectual data they provide. Learning at all levels must be adopted by mangers who understand the nature of the human spirit and that organisational learning is multi- dimensional. This multi dimensional element is not only constructed around the structural nature of the firm but also around the nature of learning. Dierkes et al (2007) describe four types of learning processes: learning-by-doing, scientific learning, learning-by-searching, and learning-by-using. This illustrate the multi faceted nature of organisational learning framework development within a firm. Managers should capitalize on task, capability, culture and individual personality to integrate mechanisms that promote and foster innovation.

At my place of work, a small volunteer based radio station, I actively encourage staff and volunteers to exchange roles and try each others activities. This results in fresh perspectives on tasks and sometimes leads to creative solutions to accepted stalemate inconveniences within our operational activities. Open and creative talking sessions allow members to share experiences and create and explore differing approaches to production, promotion or technical issues. Segmenting the stations members activities and areas of operation is counter productive in terms of the total station output. As Jennex (2008) highlights 'that for companies to achieve more effective knowledge sharing, they must move away from the paradigm of "need-to-know".'

Specializing learning mechanisms within specific departmental, regional or technological workspace helps to focus learning and innovation.McKee (1992) identifies the concept of segregated learning when exploring the firm 3M and although the firm as a diverse portfolio he rightly identifies that 'an important skill at 3M is the development and application of adhesives. This is a technological domain within which much of the organization's innovation occurs.' This area focused learning should not be exclusive to area personnel but should encourage outside participation from other organisational areas.

For me organisational learning should be part of a culture of challenging traditional and preconceived view points. Embracing the human spirit is a constructive way to promote innovation and achieve competitive advantage for the firm and the individual. While learning plays an important role in todays firm the challenges faced by managers are wide ranging and include structuring the organisation in a manner that makes learning and change a natural environment for all.

Future bonding or separating of organisational learning frameworks?

With a wide range of differing management theories and practices the question arises as how do they or can they fit together in an harmonious manner. Theories and frameworks can blend, bond or even counter other approaches. Incorporating organisational learning into this wide range of management systems and organisational structures and cultures needs careful evaluation and practical monitoring. To fully embrace organisational learning Shipton (2006) takes the approach of utalising typology as a means of categorizing and analyzing research that illustrates similarities and dissimilarities in the differing schools of thought regarding organisational learning. Because of the fast amount of data one could question how the data used could be representative over a wide range of organisational structures and belief systems. The variable factor of human psychology can influence and misguide frameworks as well as drive them forward. By using a typology approach using a comparative matrix seems to allow for managers to construct a form of understanding that could relate the their personal practical situation. By identifying the authors perspective within the matrix would allow for functional interpretation in real world environment.

Evaluation

Shiptons quadrant contexts are explored individually.

Quadrant1 – The prescriptive Perspective.

This explores the organisational learning from a practical managers perspective and identifies the concept of open visionary and all engaging approach to learning. It goes on to identify the need for more decentralized flatter organisational structures. While Shipton states that there is little empirical work to support the benefits of this form one could assume that with the growth of flatter organisations in the globalised market would support this prescriptive approach. Here we see managers fostering learning through prescriptive methods. Although form is required to guide learning into meaningful outputs I would challenge the concept that prescriptive methods are the most innovative.

Quadrant 2 – The Normative Perspective

Concerned with how we learn and how learning is guided rather than prescribed there appears to be common ground with quadrant 1. The normative approach seems more focused on the perceived or projected outcome in order to drive competitive advantage. The work is said to show that there is a smooth movement of knowledge within the normative perspective when turn over rates are low and communication is timely. Mechanisms must promote knowledge transfer and ensure that the environment of learning is maintained.

Quadrant 3 – The Explanatory Perspective

More focused on changes through organisational learning rather than the outcomes. Here we concerns around dysfunctionality of the organisational structure and a differing focus on tacit and explicit knowledge by researchers. Theoretical approaches to learning and how we engage in learning could be seen as a critical element of engaging with knowledge. However we must accept as pointed out that learning is an imperfect act that can have a cognitive and or behavioral change aspect.

Quadrant 4 – The Descriptive Perspective

Looking at learning through the eyes of academic focused on the social elements of learn we find theories rather than practicalities of organisational learning structures. Whether one choose the psychology or constructavist views we must adapt and use the information to bond with a more commercial organisational practice because of the social and psychological aspects of the individual members of the firm.

From the topology division of the research we can see that all elements overlap and can compliment each other. One of the dangerous areas for managers is to adopt single systems for learning when the target audience within the organization is made of a wide range of personalities, abilities and skills. Managers must be wary of researchers who define learning in a singular inflexible framework. Accepting the individual nature of learnis key to successful positive learning as point out by Crossan and Bedrow (2003) 'All organizations learn, for better or worse, and the challenge is to understand the pattern of organizational learning and manage it within its unique context.'

The future of organisational learning is dependent on the successful outcomes and returns that firms achieve after investing and developing learning infrastructures. This is supported by the work of Skerlavaj et al (2007) who state that 'investing effort, time and money into initiatives aimed at developing a learning-oriented culture can bring about improved performance—in terms of better relationships within and outside the company as well as in hard figures

Adapting to the needs of the future will require firms to engage in the practicalities of learning and the subsequent need to change practices to fully exploit knowledge growth. Retailers have adapted to market trends in connection with the publics desire to purchase goods online. In the UK it has involved firms learning to design and meet the needs of customers wishes. The structures employed to meet these needs as been different. Tesco's developed online systems that utilized stock from the selves of local stores while Sainsbury's responded by forming a new division to facilitate delivery.(Boddy, 2008) Learning from customers may help companies to innovate and progress but solutions to that knowledge gained may well differ

As a manager I would be inclined to adapt and fit various frameworks to meet the needs of my staff and organisation. Shipton (2006) brings the front the connections and harmonies, in general, between frameworks and theories. This is a strong confirmer that organisational learning should be an organic and evolutionary process.

Leadership

The role of the manager in a globalised organisation requires a growing number of skill sets and flexibility in approach dependent on organisational, internal and external environmental influences. The leadership skills of today's manager need to reflect rapidly changing situations and diverse cultural markets, both internal and external. For these managers the establishment of situation focused responses is critical. Adopting the right approach to the situation means the managers must be conversant with the range of theories and styles of leadership and management to get the best out of the people and departments they manage and ultimately lead. Todays manager must be a genuine person with a multi talented empathic personality able to morph around situations to foster greater learning and acceptance of new knowledge and its deployment.

The interaction between the individual and organisation in relation to learning processes must be understood. Although some may question the symbiotic relationship between the individual and organisation as illustrated by Antonacopoulou (2006) 'At the most basic level the relationship between individual and organizational level is not reciprocal' It is the nature of the individual and the collective that will determine the effectiveness and willingness for learning and the sharing and placing of the knowledge within the organisation. Approaches to learning can be divided into cognitive and behavioral and it is the complex sub divisions and the interactive play of leaders that will determine any success. Understanding the emotion of the individual and the organisation will play a major role in efficient and constructive learning. Being able to cement the elements and environments of learning is a key skill of todays managers as Leban and Zulauf (1980) point out 'Emotional intelligence combines the cognitive system, which orients us to what makes sense to the emotional system, which orients us to what matters. Good leaders should prepare for learning by developing an environment that fosters trust and security. This role of facilitating learning would fit more with organisational cultures with a low power distance ratio and a high tolerance to uncertainty as illustrated by Dierkes et al (2003). In cultures where the power distance ratio is high and the tolerance to uncertainty is low managers must take a more direct approach that directs both the individual and organisation towards a pre-determined learning objective.

Being sensitive to a firms environment and the individuals within the organisation is a critical part of developing and maintaining good learning mechanisms with strong beneficial outputs for both the individual and organisation.

Having managed many organisations over the years this week has given me the opportunity to reflect on how I have operated within different structures and how my approaches to management and in particular to the ways in which I fostered learning have changed. In the early days I can recall that my role was very much about passing on knowledge in a direct and instructive manner with very little interaction from staff. Today I tend to follow a more democratic approach that is about facilitating learning and knowledge sharing and I see myself as being part of the learning process. I am much more into the concept of lifelong learning, as I guess most of this class are as we are doing this Masters. Being a manager that says "I don't know" is today not a problem within the organisational culture I operate, however, I can see that there may be cultural environment where this would be a sign of weakness and result in a loss of respect. It is the good manager who recognizes these differences and changes their approach to meet cultural expectations and develop the learning environment around trust and respect. Whichever path we take to achieve successful learning it will come down to creating an acceptable point or area of learning. Bass (2000) stated 'The leadership in the organization has to change with the development and maturation of the organization.' I would go as far as to add the maturation of the individuals within the organisation and the more sophisticated markets. Good leaders can identify shifts in receptibilty.

Leaders must show tolerance and acceptance of all the influential areas of the individuals and organisations emotions, cultures and the varying nature of the interplay of individuals in collective environments. Applying the appropriate 'remedy' suitable to the cultural and social structure of an organisation is one of the critical skills of todays manager and leader at all levels within the organisation.

A meeting of dynamic capabilities and knowledge management.

Approaches to achieving competitive advantage and the numerous theories and framework require managers to review and utilize concepts to achieve the highest level of success. This paper will review the work of Easterby-Smith & Prieto (2008) in relationship to two specific areas, Dynamic Capabilities and Knowledge Management. Exclusive singular management theory and practice is a difficult task in a fast moving global environment that varies in terms of culture and social interaction. It therefore requires managers to engage and interact with these varying markets and environments by using theories and frameworks that better fit the operating environments.

The Relationship

The process of achieving competitive advantage can be seen on two specific levels according to Easterby-Smith & Prieto (2008). Firstly, the building of competitive advantage and secondly, the sustaining of competitive advantage. Using the theory of dynamic capabilities as a mechanism to draw on market information and the ability to reconfigure and renew existing resources would form the bases of establishing situations that lead the organisation towards competitive advantage. Knowledge management would allow managers to maintain competitive advantage by strategically placing, retaining and transferring knowledge within the organisation. It is possible under this explanation to see how the two theories can overlap and co-support each other in moving an organisation forward. The symbiotic relationship would mean that mangers could strategically plan action activity to reach the goals and market objectives of the firm.

Reviewing the relationship and interaction of the both dynamic capabilities and knowledge management the authors make a case for utalising both frameworks as tools for organisational development. Accepting that organisations work within environments the evolve rapidly and organisational structure is an evolutionary organism then adapting and the integrating of both theories would be a very strong development strategy.

While the authors highlight the emergent consensus regarding dynamic capabilities and the establishment of a distinction between dynamic and operational capabilities it is important to recognize that the practicalities of each of the theories allow for managers to evolve progress paths and generate solutions based on knowledge acquisition and management. The whole relationship from fostering and harvesting customer knowledge and embodying procedures and routines into the dynamic structure of the organisation seems to naturally lend itself to strategic knowledge management and achieving sustainable competitive advantage. We can see the relationship between gathering knowledge from a dynamic market and the transfer of that knowledge, both tacit and explicit, through structured processes that clearly identify the needs of each form of knowledge. Easterby-Smith & Prieto (2008) exploration of the contrasting forms of knowledge highlights the need for key sources for efficient management and control. Apart from identifying the role of management processes they also highlight the importance of IT infrastructures and associated activities and resources.This is supported by Sher and Lee (2004) 'IT dimensions of KM have been shown to be important for enhancing dynamic capabilities'. While this is a critical part of the control and distribution of knowledge and the instigation of learning systems it must be understood that the fostering of creativity and innovation is a vital part of achieving efficient knowledge management.

The role of dynamic capabilities and knowledge management.

We can see the interplay between dynamic capabilities and knowledge management theories and the authors explore the overlapping nature of the two areas. It would seem that the use of these systems together offers managers a path to achieve longterm strategic goals through organisation learning, providing managers do not lose sight of the need for fast reactive strategies using alternative processes when organisational situations demand. Easterby-Smith & Prieto (2008) confirmation of Zollo and Winter (2002) concept that exploration and exploitation are critical parts of achieving competitive advantage. The recognition of going outside the organisation to gather knowledge for internal exploitation fits well within the bonding of dynamic capabilities and knowledge management practices.

The authors show a strong link between learning processes in the organisation and its knowledge management. I would accept that the concepts of dynamic capabilities and knowledge management meet and indeed overlap and offer organisations critical route and systems for achieving competitive advantage. The authors exploration results in a strong case for using in harmonious processes both theories and I would concur that it seems a very practical rote for mangers to take. In fact it could be argued that dynamic capabilities become much less effective if knowledge management doesn't come into play as concluded by Nielsen (2006) 'emphasis on dynamic capabilities is of little value if the knowledge management activities are not taken into account as well.'

There must of course be a continuous assessment of the implementation of theories in the 'real world' and by its very nature the global market evolves and adapts rapidly and therefore refinement and advancement of theories and frameworks must continue. organisational survival is paramount and it is only by learning to improve learning mechanisms will the future successes be sustainable. Even within the same industry there is going to be gaps in knowledge as pointed out by Cepeda and Vera (2007) 'the depth and breadth of knowledge resources varies across firms competing in the same industry' and it is the firm hat stays ahead in dynamic capability and knowledge management process that will gain the most

Knowledge Transfer

The knowledge transfer and learning systems of traditional SME's are restricted by the very nature of their structure and ownership. When owner – managers control firms there is naturally a lack of two way communication structures, owners seem to ensure that there is a strong hierarchical environment that flows data, instructions and objectives down the line. While this may work in some cases, the owner remaining a controlling focal point, it does lead to low organisational learning levels and fosters inefficiencies. For SME's to meet the manufacturing standards and efficiencies required by larger customers who practice supply auditing they must engage in ways to learn as an organisation and implement systems that drive, through organisational learning, the firm towards being able to compete globally. Jones and Macpherson (2006) look at the practical way in which three SME's where able, in partnership with external resources, to move towards implementing internal learning systems and practices that enabled them to retain and develop relationships with key customers.

The Jones and Macpherson (2006) paper explores the development relationships and needs of three SME's and their need to change processes in order to maintain and increase key customers in a changing efficiency driven market. The view that owner – managers tend to foster a controlling environment while not possessing key skills and or internal structures to pass on, deliver or acquire skills and knowledge needed to compete effectively stands well within the traditional SME structure. Jones and Macpherson (2006) identify this lack 'Many SMEs operating in mature sectors lack the skills and knowledge to adopt modern management techniques and new technologies.'The papers direct feedback from the firms owner managers illustrate that their lack of key skills and identifies the need to evolve their operations to meet their customers needs stands out.

By accepting shortfalls in knowledge and skills each of the firms embark on instigating external resources to foster learning and organisational process changes. This can be a difficult task for some owner managers because it does mean a certain amount of power relinquishing in order to promote sharing and foster learning cultures within the firm. Once owner managers overcome the fear of transferring control and some power to the body of the organisation and accept that there are sources of information and practices outside of the organisation they can then begin to move the firm forward. Natural resistance can hinder the firm and it is only when dramatic events open the eyes of managers that action is taken. I would propose that all SME owner managers should embark on similar routes before the crisis occurs. This will allow for a stronger firm more able to meet the demands of its customers. This ability or willingness to foster a policy absorptive capacity will as illustrated by the authors leads to competitive advantage through strong focused strategical development and renewal. This function of external resources shows that there is vital developmental advantage to stepping out of the organisational box as pointed out by Jones (2006) Change agents are particularly important in assisting others to recognize the benefits of adopting new ways of working.

The papers exploration of organisational learning and strategic renewal illustrates well the need to embark on the implementation of learning systems, however, as mentioned earlier one of the key problems for SME's is the potential resistance of owner managers to relinquish control or power. The possibility of failure may trigger movement to establishing the systems required for survival, but also, the larger established firms who require the SME as a supplier may find it beneficial to establish mentoring teams to assist in organisational change as Lucas Aerospace did in the paper.

This need to change for future survival was also highlighted by Choueke and Armstrong (1998) when the said that firms needed to respond to changing environments and listen to customers.

Team Performance

Learning within an organisations global structure poses several problems for managers. They are faced with the dilemma of creating fixed corporate learning structures or localised structures that fully accommodate regional social and cultural variances. However, MNC's need to foster consistency across the firms global presence in terms of its knowledge management and learning mechanisms. Zellmer-Bruhn and Gibson (2006) explore this conflict within their exploration of the MNC macro team context in relation to learning efficiencies.

Their studies, in part, look at the integration of practices across the organisation and the influencing factors at more local levels to achieve the most appropriate structures for a MNC. The concept that a single format structure works across an entire global organisation falls down because of its lack in accountability of regional, social, cultural and market influencers. The reliance of subsidiaries or regional department focus on singular local learning development systems will segregate the department from the corporate overview and risk establishing a myopic approach to strategic development. Zellmer-Bruhn and Gibson (2006) highlight that the balance between the two approaches key to the MNC's success. By balancing the needs of the global organisation against the local influencers to learning a firm is much better suited to compete competitively in a global market. The balanced approach also allows for a better multi flow of knowledge required to promote creativity and innovation as pointed out by McGill, Slocum Jr and Lei (1992) 'Innovation occurs in each local market and learning flows in many different directions.' The more harmonized team learning will allow for innovation and creativity within the frame of a global strategy. In fact the setting of corporate boundaries may well focus innovation and foster greater creativity within the team and enhance performance. It would seem from the paper that the engagement of a strategy of embedding a bigger picture into a local environment is a model best suited to today's MNC, however one could argue that it would be more beneficial to adopt a singular approach that bypasses the need for the inclusion of local factors, thus creating a single message and structure that could be more effectively implemented and measured across the entire firm and removing the risk of local contamination to teams and their learning environments.

The link between team learning and performance goes side by side not only in fostering good learning practices and innovative translation of that process but also by bonding teams into a collective force powered by a corporate vision. The bond between learning and performance is tied to the development of trust between team members and once trust is established performance through innovation is enhanced. This positioning of trust development is supported by Erdem,Ozen and Atsan (2003) 'trust can be seen as a necessary underpinning.' Firms should understand the collective power of accumulated knowledge and its ability to push the firm forward on a global scale. The use of knowledge within a team on all levels of operation is the driving force to success.

Alliance Trust

When firms embark on international partnerships and alliances there usually is a clear strategic reason for the partnership. It is the mechanisms that are put in place to facilitate the partnership that determine the outcome of the partnership. Using the alliance as a means to mutually move the partners toward competitive advantage becomes reliant on how information, knowledge and communications are handled. The specific need to innovate in a fast moving global market place will place a significant burden on the partnership, especially if the partnership is new. Dierkes et al (2006) identify this fragility of international strategic alliances. Mangers must establish sensitivities to this environment and put in place structures and communication strategies to facilitate understanding and trust. Nielsen & Nielsen (2009) exploration of the utalisation and exchange of tacit knowledge between international alliances and how trust influences its innovative outcomes draws on some interesting concepts in terms of the inter firm relationship development and the resulting innovative outcomes.

It is how firms see each other that can determine the flow of tacit knowledge. This flow will impact on the ability of the firm to innovate. If levels of exchange and exploration are low then this may result in poor movement towards competitive advantage. The creating of a safe sharing environment will help in learning and knowledge transfer. Nielsen & Nielsen (2009) show that the relationship between trust and learning from tacit knowledge is a sensitive area for international alliances, especially when cultural and social environments could offer barriers to understanding, exchange and the fostering of trust.

Explicit mechanisms for mediating between organisations is going to be a key role for managers in order to encourage the development of trust and the free flow of tacit knowledge. Not to do this will lead to slow inter firm relationship development and poor or no innovation. Nielsen &

Nielsen (2009) do point out that learning is not the only factor in ensuring innovation and this is true, it maybe that learning and the exchange of tacit knowledge is not enough to develop new outputs but it is the environment that nurtures the growth of the embryonic formation of both inputs. The nurturing of learning is a key ingredient to productive innovation. The challenge is creating that close nurturing environment and as Inkpen (1998) says Properly managed, alliances can yield new and valuable insights that can lead to tangible performance improvements.

During my time as the CEO of a start up airline we embarked on establishing several international alliances and partnerships. The transfer of knowledge would have been more beneficial to my firm and as a result of this imbalance we uncounted various levels of uncertainty of motives from both ourselves and our partners. I think that this was due to the lack of understanding of each others partnership objectives outside of the key commercial targets. The question of 'why us' as partners seemed to rear it head on more than one occasion. This lack of understanding and hence trust hindered the development of the partnership and my firm. The development and establishment of trust at all levels is beneficial in tacit knowledge exchange, learning and innovation that leads to competitive advantage.

Through the paper by Nielsen & Nielsen (2009) we can see the relationship between tacit knowledge exchange, learning and trust playing an important role promoting alliance innovation although this is only one set of ingredients needed to take the alliance forward in terms of competitive advantage through innovation. Key to the success of the alliance is embedding environments that account for cultural, social and operational systems differences in a manner the brings the uniqueness of each firm into one common comfortable area for the growth of trust and understanding.

Barriers

Organisational learning offers firms a route to competitive advantage, however, barriers emerge within the deployment of learning systems and knowledge management. These barriers need to be addressed and removed by managers in order to sustain a level of knowledge and learning quality. The identification of specific barriers within the organisation should be identified by managers and may vary dependent on the cultural, social and individual attitudes and actions.

The variety of obstacles and the relationship to organisational structure as been explored by Schilling and Kluge (2009) using the 4I framework of intuiting, interpreting, integrating and institutionalizing as a method of evaluating barrier impacts and solutions. Using this particular approach would seem to account for the social psychological restrictions to learning within the environment of the entire learning and knowledge management structure. A clear approach to the specific causes of resistance and the need for managers to find ways of channelling the resistance to more productive and constructive outcomes can be derived from the understanding of the core instigators within each of the 4I areas. It seems that while there are identification processes with in each environment the over all identification of barriers is at an organizational level is complex but at individual levels key recognized psychological influencers can be identified and methods used to overcome resistance and empower the individual to accept and participate in learning processes. The ability of a firm to overcome barriers will depend on the leadership within the firm. Leadership should play a vital role in guiding structures and staff towards beneficial learning, although, the area of leadership within barriers to learning is described by Dierkes et al (2006) as a 'fuzzy notion' it would still be instrumental in establishing a cultural environment of acceptance.

The presence of the key area and environment needed for organisational learning such as trust, good management, free flowing communication will all help overcome barriers. It is when the factors in these areas is lacking within the organisation that the growth of resistance is seen. Schilling and Kluge (2009) identify several short falls in these areas and that within the 4I framework there is evidence of interconnecting and relating factors that can hinder or damage organisational learning.

Managers should look at all factors including: innovation itself, employees' mindsets, skills and motivation, group dynamics, leadership, organizational structure and culture as well as political activities as identified by Schilling and Kluge (2009) when establishing learning mechanisms and systems. Dierkes et al (2006) support the concept of diverse scenarios for barrier creation within organisations and it is clear that the balance between organisational structures and personal social and cultural influencers and finely balanced. Unbalancing the environment will lead to barrier creation and a dis-harmonious organisational environment.

Within in my current organisation we recently employed a training co ordinator who's role was to ensure volunteers gained from learning and sharing skills, both tacit and explicit. Surprisingly we came up against some resistance to attending training sessions. After further investigation we came across several reasons for non attendance: 1. "I know all I need to know to do my job" 2. A reluctance to show a lack of skills, especially in explicit areas. 3. A fear that more knowledge, like editing skills would mean more work. All of these individual reasons for avoidance with a little understanding and guidance. Group 1& 2 were encouraged to share/transfer their knowledge within the group by being facilitators and group 3 were informed that additional knowledge did not equate to more work. Resulting in high training session attendance and greater knowledge sharing.

Identification of barriers and there causes before or early on in the organisational learning development process is vital in order not to establish hard to reverse cultural habits within the knowledge management systems.

References

Adler and Kwon (2002) SOCIALCAPITALP:ROSPECTSFOR A NEW CONCEPT Academy of Management Review,Vol.27,No. 1, 17-40.

Alesina and Perotti (1996) Fiscal Discipline and the Budget Process The American Economic Review, Vol. 86, No. 2, Papers and Proceedings of the Hundredth and Eighth Annual Meeting of the American Economic Association San Francisco, CA, January 5-7, 1996 pp. 401-407

Alavi and Leidner (2001) Knowledge Management and Knowledge Management Systems: Conceptual Foundations and Research Issues. MIS Quarterly, Vol. 25, No. 1, pp. 107-136

Ambler, T & Styles C (1996). Brand development versus new product development: towards a process model of extension decisions Marketing Intelligence & Planning 14/7 pp10–19

Anandarajan A and Wen H.J.(1999) Evaluation of information technology investment. Management Decision 37/4 pp 329-337

Andrews and Chompusr (2001) Lessons in 'Cross-Vergenc Restructuring the Thai Subsidiary Corporation. Journal of International Business Studies, Vol. 32, No. 1 , pp. 77-93

Anon, BBC News (2007) BSkyB agrees £125m Amstrad deal

Antonacopoulou E.P (2006) The Relationship between Individual and Organizational Learning: New Evidence from Managerial Learning Practices. Management Learning. Vol. 37(4): pp455–473

Atkinson D.(n.d) Thinking The Art of Management Stepping into 'Heidegger's Shoes' EBook Palgrave Macmillan

Aubert C. Rey P. & Kovaic W. (2003) The Impact of Leniency Programs on Cartels

Avlonitis, G. J., & Indounas, K. A. (2005) 'Pricing objectives and pricing methods in the services sector', The Journal of Services Marketing, 19 (1), pp. 47–57.

Bal and Foster (2000) Managing the virtual team and controlling effectiveness. International Journal of Production Research VOL.38, NO.17, 4019±4032

Bass B.M. (2000) The Future of Leadership in Learning Organizations. Journal of Leadership & Organizational Studies 2000 7: 18

Becker S and Green D. Jr (1962) Budgeting and Employee Behavior The Journal of Business, Vol. 35, No. 4 pp. 392-402

Berthon, P., Holbrook, M. B., & Hulbert, J. M. (2003) 'Understanding and managing the brand space', MIT Sloan Management Review, 44 (2), pp. 49–54.

Bird, A. & Fang, T. (2009) 'Editorial: cross cultural management in the age of globalization', International Journal of Cross Cultural Management, 9 (2), pp. 139–142, Sage Premier Database

Brand A (1998) Journal of Knowledge Management Volume 2 Number 1 September 1998

Brett, J., Behfar, K. & Kern, M. (2006) 'Managing multicultural teams', Harvard Business Review, 84 (11), pp.84-91, Business Source Premier

Broddy, D. (2008) Management An introduction Harlow, Essex: Pearson Education

Bruggemann W. and Slagmulder R. (1995) The impact on technological change on management accounting. Management Accounting Research 6, pp 241-252

Burns J. and Scapens R.W (2000) Conceptualizing management accounting change: an institutional framework. Management Accounting Research,11, pp3-25

Caramazza, F., Ricci, L. & Salgado, R. (2004) 'International financial contagion in currency crises', Journal of International Money and Finance, 23 (1), February, pp. 51–70.

Carkovik M. and Levine R (n.d) Does foreign direct investment accelerate growth

Caulkins D. & Weiner E. (1998) Finding a Work Culture that Fits: Egalitarian Manufacturing Firms in Mid Wales. Anthropology of work review vol:19 iss:1 pg:27

Cepeda and Vera (2007) Dynamic capabilities and operational capabilities: A knowledge management perspective. Journal of Business Research 60 pp 426–437

Chenhall R.H. and Morris D. (1986) The Impact of Structure, Environment, and Interdependence on the Perceived Usefulness of Management Accounting Systems. The Accounting Review, Vol. 61, No. 1 pp. 16-35

Chi-Kuo Mao, (n.d)Principles of Human Organization Change, Institute of Business and Management, National Chiao-Tung University, Taiwan

Child, J. (2005) Organization: contemporary principles and practice. Malden, MA: Blackwell Publishing.

Chevrier, S. (2009) 'Is national culture still relevant to management in a global context? The case of Switzerland', International Journal of Cross Cultural Management, 9 (2), pp.169–181, Sage Journals

Choueke R. and Armstrong R. (1998) The learning organisation in small and medium-sized enterprises - A destination or a journey? Inte Jnl of Entrepreneurial Behaviour & Research, Vol. 4 No. 2, pp. 129-140.

Christensen C.M. and Bower J.L. (1996) Customer Power, Strategic Investment, and the Failure of Leading Firms. Strategic Management Journal, Vol. 17, No. 3 pp. 197-218

Cook P and Kirkpatrick C. (1995) Globalization, Regionalization and Third World Development. Regional Studies, Vol. 31.1, pp. 55± 66

Cook, Sarah. Change Management Excellence : Using the Four Intelligences for Successful Organizational Change. London, , GBR: Kogan Page, Limited, 2004.

Crainer, Stuart. Greatest Management Decisions Ever Made. Saranac Lake, NY, USA: AMACOM, 1999. p 206.

Crossan M.M and Bedrow I. (2003) ORGANIZATIONAL LEARNING AND STRATEGIC RENEWAL. Strategic Management Journal , 24: pp1087–1105

Dean A.M. (2002) "Service quality in call centres: implications for customer loyalty" Managing Service Quality Vol 12 No 6 pp414-423 (Online) www.emeraldinsight.com (Accessed 4th June 2009)

Dell, M (1999) Direct from Dell: Strategies that revolutionized an industry, Harper Business, New York

Dierkes, M., Berthoin Antal, A., Child, J. & Nonaka, I., eds. (2003) Handbook of organizational learning and knowledge. Oxford: Oxford University Press.

Drucker, P,F (1999) 'Managing Non-Profit organisation.' Butterworth-Heinemann, Oxford

Easterby-Smith, M. & Prieto, I. (2008) 'Dynamic capabilities and knowledge management: an integrative role for learning', British Journal of Management, 19 (3), pp. 235-249, EBSCOhost Business Source Premier

Ehin C (2008) Journal of Intellectual Capital Vol. 9 No. 3, pp. 337-350 q Emerald Group Publishing Limited

Elkins D.J. and Simeon R.E.B (1979) A Cause in Search of Its Effect, or What Does Political Culture Explain? Comparative Politics, Vol. 11, No. 2, pp. 127-145

Ely and Thomas (2001) Cultural Diversity at Work: The Effects of Diversity Perspectives on Work Group Processes and Outcomes. Administrative Science Quarterly, Vol. 46, No. 2 , pp. 229-273

Erdem,F. Ozen J. and Atsan N. (2003) The relationship between trust and team performance. Work Study Volume 52 . Number 7 .. pp. 337-340

Epple D.(1987) Hedonic Prices and Implicit Markets: Estimating Demand and Supply Functions for Differentiated Products.The Journal of Political Economy, Vol. 95, No. 1 pp. 59-80

Fidrmuc J. & Korhonen I. (2009) The impact of the global financial crisis on business cycles in Asian emerging economies. Journal of Asian Economics

Fogliatto F.S & da Silveira G.J.C(2008) Mass customization: A method for market segmentation and choice menu design, Int. J. Production Economics 111 pp606–622 (on-line)

Foss N.J & Klein P.G (2004) Entrepreneurship and the Economic Theory of the Firm: Any Gains from Trade? Handbook of Entrepreneurship: Disciplinary Perspectives

Frahm J and Brown K (2007) First steps: linking change communication to change receptivity. Journal of Organizational Change Management Vol. 20 No. 3,

Frazier G.L. (1999)   Organizing and Managing Channels of Distribution. Marketing Science. Volume 27, No. 2, pages 226-240.

Freedman D.A (2004) Graphical Models for Causation, and the Identification Problem. EVALUATION REVIEW, Vol. 28 No. 4, pp267-293

García-Martos, C. Rodríguez, J and Sánchez M, J. (2007) Mixed Models for Short-Run Forecasting of Electricity Prices: Application for the Spanish Market IEEE TRANSACTIONS ON POWER SYSTEMS, VOL. 22, NO. 2,

Ghauri, P. & Fang, T. (1999) The Chinese business negotiation process: a socio-cultural analysis

Gibbons, R. (1998) 'Incentives in organizations' The Journal of Economic Perspectives, 12 (4) pp. 115–132.

Giovannucci (n.d) Basic Trade Finance Tools: Payment Methods in International Trade. A Guide to Developing Agricultural Markets and Agro-enterprises.

Gittell, Jody Hoffer. Southwest Airlines Way : The Power of Relationships for Superior Performance. Blacklick, OH, USA: McGraw-Hill Trade, 2002.

Goldkuhl G & Lind M (2008) Coordination and transformation in business processes: towards an integrated view, Business Process Management Journal Vol. 14 No. 6, pp. 761-777

Goldman S.L Nagel, R.N. Davison B. and Schmid P.D.(2009) Next Generation Agility: Smart Business and Smart Communities.

Gomez P.J., Cespedes-Lorente. & Valle-Cabrera J,R. (2005) Organizational learning capability: a proposal of measurement. Journal of Business Research 58 pp715–725

Gonzlez, A. M., & Bello, L. (2002) 'The construct "lifestyle" in market segmentation: The behaviour of tourist consumers', European Journal of Marketing, 36 (1/2), pp. 51–85.

Graham J.R and Harvey C.R (2001) The theory and practice of corporate finance: evidence from the field. Journal of Financial Economics 60 pp187-243

Graeff, T. R., & Harmon, S. (2002) 'Collecting and using personal data: consumers' awareness and concerns', Journal of Consumer Marketing, 19 (4/5), pp. 302–318.

Granlund M.(2001) Towards explaining stability in and around management accounting systems. Management Accounting Research, 12, pp 141–166

Grant R.M.(1991) The Resource-Based Theory of Competitive Advantage: Implications for Strategy. California Management Review; pg. 114

Grant (1996) Toward a Knowledge-Based Theory of the Firm. Strategic Management Journal, Vol. 17, Special Issue: Knowledge and the Firm pp. 109-122

Grantham L.M (1997) The validity of the product life cycle in the high-tech industry. Marketing Intelligence & Planning 15/1 pp4-19

Griswold W. (1999) Cultures and Societies in a Changing World. AI & Soc 13: pp446-449

Grosse R and Behrman J.N. (1992) Theory in international businessTransnational Corporations, vol. I, no. I , pp. 93-126.

Gupta, M. & Kohli, A. (2006) ' Enterprise resource planning systems and its implications for operations function', Technovation, 26 (5), pp. 687-696, Elsevier Science Direct

Hall   H(2001) Social exchange for knowledge exchange. Managing knowledge: conversations and critiques, University of Leicester Management Centre,

Hammer M, (2001) The Superefficient Company HARVARD BUSINESS REVIEW

Haskel, J.E., Pereira, S.C. & Slaughter, M.J. (2007) 'Does inward foreign direct investment boost the productivity of domestic firms?', Review of Economics & Statistics, 89 (3), August, pp. 482–496.

Hauner D. (2002) The Euro, the Dollar, and the International Monetary System. The Economics of Regional Trade Agreements. Federal Ministry of Finance.

Heath C. (1995) Escalation and de-escalation of commitment in response to sunk costs: The role of budgeting in mental accounting. Organisational behaviour and human decision processes. Vol 62 No1 pp38-54

van Heck, E. & Vervest, P. (2007) 'Smart business networks: how the network wins', Communications of the ACM, 50 (6), pp. 28-37, The Guide to Computing Literature

Heikkilä J. (2002) From supply to demand chain management: efficiency and customer satisfaction. Journal of Operations Management 20 pp 747–767

Higgins-Desbiolles (2006) Another world is possible: Tourism, globalisation and the responsible alternative. Australian Digital Theses Program.

Humby, C (2004). Scoring Points : How Tesco Is Winning Customer Loyalty.London, , GBR: Kogan Page, Limited, 2004. p 160.

Hurn, B.J. (2007) 'The influence of culture on international business negotiations', Industrial and Commercial Training, 39(7), pp. 354-360,

Inglehart R. and Baker W.E. (2000) Modernization, Cultural Change, and the Persistence of Traditional Values. American Sociological Review, Vol. 65, No. 1, Looking Forward, Looking Back: Continuity and Change at the Turn of the Millenium, pp. 19-51

Inkpen A.C.(1998) Learning and knowledge acquisition through international strategic

alliances. Academy of Management Executive,Vol. 12, No. 4

Jain S.C (1989) Standardization of International Marketing Strategy: Some Research Hypotheses

The Journal of Marketing, Vol. 53, No. 1 pp. 70-79

Jaiswal A.K (2008) Customer satisfaction and service quality measurement in Indian call centres. Managing Service Quality Vol. 18 No. 4, pp405-416

Johnston R.(1999) Management theory; Operations management; Service operations. International Journal of Operations & Production Management Vol 19 No 2 pp: 104-124

Jarvenpaa S.L and Ives B. (1994) The Global Network Organization of the Future: Information Management Opportunities and Challenges. Journal of Management Information Systems, Vol. 10, No. 4, pp. 25-57

Jennex M. (2008) Current Issues in Knowledge Management, INFORMATION SCIENCE REFERENCE. Hershey • New York

Jones, O. (2006) 'Developing absorptive capacity in mature organizations: the change agent's role', Management Learning, 37 (3), pp. 355-376, SAGE Premier

Jones, O. & Macpherson, A. (2006) 'Inter-organizational learning and strategic renewal in SMEs: extending the 4I network', Long Range Planning, 39 (2), pp. 155-175, Elsevier ScienceDirect

Kacem J.J & Lee J.A.(2002) "The Influence of Culture on Consumer Impulsive Buying Behaviour" Journal of Consumer Psychology, Vol. 12, No. 2 pp. 163-176

Kamien M.I. Muller E. & Zang I. (1992) Joint Ventures and R&D Cartels The American Economic Review, Vol. 82, No. 5 pp. 1293-1306

Kaminsky & Reinhart (1998) On Crises, Contagion, and Confusion. The Duke University conference "Globalization, Capital Market Crises and Economic Reform."

Kaplan, R.S. and Norton, D.P. (2006) 'How to Implement a New Strategy Without Disrupting Your Organization', Harvard Business Review 84 (3) pp. 100-109

Kara A. & Kaynak E. (1997) Markets of a single customer: exploiting conceptual developments in market segmentation. European Journal of Marketing, Vol. 31 No. 11/12, 1997, pp. 873-895.

Kasurinen T (2001) Influence of the Implementation Process on Management Accounting Change in a Hierarchical Corporation. L T A 4 / 0 1 • P . 459– 4 7 9

Kauffman & Wang (2008) Tuning into the digital channel: evaluating business model characteristics for Internet firm survival. Inf Technol Manage 9:pp 215–232

Keen, P.G.W. and Knapp, E.M. (1996), Every Manager's Guide to Business Processes: a Glossary of Key Terms and Concepts for Today's Business Leaders, Harvard Business School Press, Boston, MA.

Kelley, L., MacNab, B. & Worthley, R. (2006) 'Crossvergence and cultural tendencies: a longitudinal test of the Hong Kong, Taiwan and United States banking sectors', Journal of International Management, 12 (1), pp. 67–84, Science Direct

Kotler, P., & Keller, K. L. (2009) Marketing Management (International Student). 13th ed. Upper Saddle River, NJ: Pearson Education.

Lancaster G. (2004) "The influence of employee characteristics on market orientation" The International Journal of Bank Marketing Vol. 22 No. 5, pp. 343-365

Langfred, C,W and Moye, N,A (2004) 'Effects of Task Autonomy on Performance: An Extended Model Considering Motivational, Informational, and Structural Mechanisms' Journal of Applied Psychology , Vol. 89, No. 6, 934–945

Lafferty, B. A., & Hult, G. T. M. (2001) 'A synthesis of contemporary market orientation perspectives', European Journal of Marketing, 35 (1/2), pp. 92–109.

Laiken M (2001) MODELS OF ORGANIZATIONAL LEARNING: PARADOXES AND BEST PRACTICES IN THE POST INDUSTRIAL WORKPLACE. The research network for New Approaches to Lifelong Learning. NALL Working Paper # 25

Leban W. and Zulauf C.(1980) Linking emotional intelligence abilities and transformational leadership styles. The Leadership & Organization Development Journal Vol. 25 No. 7, pp. 554-564

Lee, M.R. (2009) 'E-ethical leadership for virtual project teams', International Journal of Project Management, 27 (5), pp.456-463.

Lindert P.H.and WIlliamson J.G. (2001) DOES GLOBALIZATION MAKE THE WORLD MORE UNEQUAL? NBER Globalization in Historical Perspective conference in Santa Barbara, California, May 3-6,

Linn S.E (2004) "Food Marketing to Children in the Context of a Marketing Maelstrom" Journal of Public Health Policy, Vol. 25, No. 3/4 , pp. 367-378

Listerman R.A, and Romesberg J. (2009) "Are we safe yet" Strategic Finance- July pp27-33

Meldrum M.J.(1995) Marketing high-tech products:the emerging themes. European Journal of Marketing Vol. 29 No. 10, pp. 45-58.

Ljungberg, J. (1997), "From workflow to conversation", PhD thesis, Department of Informatics, Go¨teborg University, Go¨teborg.

Lo B.W.N & Kao F.J (2008) Variation in Country-Based Ranking Lists Among Consumers' Choices of Top E-Commerce Web Sites: Implications for International E-Marketing International Journal of Business and Information Volume 3, Number 3,

López, S.P., Peón, J.M.M. & Ordás, C.J.V. (2005) 'Organizational learning as a determining factor in business performance', The Learning Organization, 12 (3), pp. 227-245, Emerald

Luo, Y and Shenkar, O. (2006) The multinational corporation as a multilingual community: Language and organization in a global context. Journal of International Business Studies 37, pp321–339

Madon S. (1997) Information-Based Global Economy and Socioeconomic Development:

The Case of Bangalore. The Information Society, 13:pp227±243

Marchhington M. &Wilkinson, A. (2008) Human resource management at work, People management and development. 4th ed, London, England: Chartered Institute of Personnel Development.

Martinsons M. Davison R. Tse D. (1999) The balanced scorecard: a foundation for the strategic management of information systems. Decision Support Systems 25 71–88

Maxwell N. (2000) "A new conception of science" Physics World August 17-18

McAdam Mason and Josephine McCrory (2007) Exploring the dichotomies within the tacit knowledge literature: towards a process of tacit knowing in organizations. JOURNAL OF KNOWLEDGE MANAGEMENT VOL. 11 NO. 2 pp. 43-59,

McGill, M.E Slocum Jr J.W. and Lei D. (1992) Management practices in learning organizations. Organizational Dynamics Volume 21, Issue 1, pp 5-17

McKee D. (1992) An Organizational Learning Approach to Product Innovation. Journal of Product Innovation Management. Volume 9, Issue 3

Mead, R. & Andrews, T.G. (2009) International management. 4th ed. Chichester, England: John Wiley & Sons.

de Mello Jr L.R.(1999) "Foreign direct investment led growth: evidence from time series and panel data.Oxford Economic paper 51 pp133-155

Metcalf, L.E., Shankarmahesh, M., Bird, A., Lituchy, T.R. & Peterson, M.F. (2007) 'Cultural influences in negotiations: a four country comparative analysis' International Journal of Cross Cultural Management, 7 (2), pp.147–168, Sage Journals

Mizeski R.W. Golden L.L. Kernan J.B. (1979) " The Attribution Process in Consumer Decision Making" The Journal of Consumer Research, Vol. 6, No. 2, Special Issue on Consumer Decision Making, pp. 123-140

Nelson, R. R.(2008)'Economic Development from the Perspective of Evolutionary Economic Theory',Oxford Development Studies,36:1,9 — 21

Nerreklit (2000) The balance on the balanced scorecard- a critical analysis of some of its assumptions Management Accounting Research, 11, pp 65-88

Nenes, G. Panagiotidou, S. & Tagaras G.(2010) Inventory management of multiple items with irregular demand: A case study. European Journal of Operational Research 205 pp313–324.

Ng J.M.J (2009) Barriers to e-commerce policy in logistics: an exploratory study of the Pearl

River Delta, China. International Journal of Logistics Research and Applications

Nielsen A.P (2006) Understanding dynamic capabilities through knowledge management. JOURNAL OF KNOWLEDGE MANAGEMENT VOL. 10 NO. 4 pp. 59-71

Nielsen, B.B. & Nielsen, S. (2009) 'Learning and innovation in international strategic alliances: an empirical test of the role of trust and tacitness', Journal of Management Studies, 46 (6), pp. 1031-1056,

Nonaka, Toyama and Konno (2000) SECI, Ba and Leadership: a Unified Model of Dynamic Knowledge Creation. Long Range Planning Volume 33, Issue 1, 1 pp 5-34

Nonaka, I. & von Krogh, G. & Voelpel, S.C. (2006) 'Organizational knowledge creation theory: evolutionary paths and future advances', Organization Studies, 27 (8), pp. 1179-1208, Sage Premier 2009

Oosthuizen, T. (2004) 'In marketing across cultures: are you enlightening the world or are you speaking in tongues?', Design Issues, 20 (2), 61–72, MIT Press Journals

Oviatt, B.M. & McDougall,P.P. (1994) 'Toward a theory of international new ventures', Journal of International Business Studies, 25 (1), pp. 45–64.

Palich L.E & Gomez-Mejia L.R (1999) A Theory of Global Strategy and Firm Efficiencies: Considering the Effects of Cultural Diversity. Journal of Management 25; 587

Palmisano, S.J. (2006) 'The globally integrated enterprise', Foreign Affairs, 85 (3), pp. 127-136, EBSCOhost Business Source Premier

Pan, S . Chon K. and Song H.(2009)" Visualizing Tourism Trends: A Combination of ATLAS.ti and BiPlot." Journal of Travel Research; 46; 339

Panzar J.C and Willig R.D (1977) Economies of Scale in Multi-Output Production

The Quarterly Journal of Economics, Vol. 91, No. 3 pp. 481-493

Paper and Chang (2005) The State of Business Process Reengineering: A Search for Success Factors. Total Quality Management Vol. 16, No. 1, 121–133,

Park Y.J. (2008) "Privacy regime, culture and user practices in the cyber-marketplace" INFO VOL. 10 NO. 2, pp. 57-74,

Parker D. (1999) Regulating public utilities: lessons from the UK experience. International Review of Administrative Sciences

Peltokorpi V. Nonaka I. and Kodama M. (2007) NTT DoCoMo's Launch of I-Mode in the Japanese Mobile Phone Market: A Knowledge Creation Perspective. Journal of Management Studies 44:1

Peng, M.W., Wang, D.Y.L. & Jiang, Y. (2008) 'An institution-based view of international business strategy: A focus on emerging economies', Journal of International Business Studies, 39 (5), July/August, pp. 920–936.

Phelps N.A. and Tewdwr-Jones M.(2001) Globalisation, Regions and the State: Exploring the Limitations of Economic Modernisation through Inward Investment Urban Studies, Vol. 38, No. 8, pp1253–1272,

Pollak R.A. and Wales T.J.(1981) Demographic Variables in Demand Analysis. Econometrica, Vol. 49, No. 6, pp. 1533-1551

Ralston, D.A. (2007) 'The crossvergence perspective: reflections and projections', Journal of International Business Studies, 39 (1), pp. 27–40, Palgrave Macmillan

Ralston (2008) The crossvergence perspective: reflections and projections. Journal of International Business Studies 39, 27–40

Ramirez (n.d) SAM - The 3-Part Process of Social Media Marketing, American Salesman

Reinhart C.M & Roghoff K.S (2008) IS THE 2007 U.S. SUB-PRIME FINANCIAL CRISIS SO DIFFERENT? AN INTERNATIONAL HISTORICAL COMPARISON. NBER WORKING PAPER SERIES

Richardson K. A.(2008) "Managing Complex Organisations: Complexity Thinking and Science and Art Management" E:CO Issue Vol 10 No 2 p17

Roberts, John (2004) The Modern Firm Organizational design and performance, Oxford: Oxford University Press.

Roberts P.W and Amit R. (2003) The Dynamics of Innovative Activity and Competitive Advantage: The Case of Australian Retail Banking, Organization Science, Vol. 14, No. 2 pp. 107-122

Ross & Sennyey (2008) The Library is Dead, Long Live the Library! The Practice of Academic Librarianship and the Digital Revolution.The Journal of Academic Librarianship. Volume 34, Issue 2, Pages 145-152

Salvatore, D. (2007) Managerial economics – Principles and worldwide applications. 6th ed. New York: Oxford University Press

Scapens, R.W. (2006) 'Understanding management accounting practices: a personal journey', The British Accounting Review, 38 (1), pp. 1–30, Elsevier SD Freedom Collection

Schuiling, I. & Kapferer, J.-N. (2004) 'Executive insights: Real differences

between local and international brands: Strategic implications for international

marketers', Journal of International Marketing, 12 (4), pp. 97–112.

Seng Woo H. and Prud'homme, C. (1999) Cultural characteristics prevalent in the Chinese negotiation process. European Business Review Volume: 99 Number: 5 pp: 313-322

Shapira Z and Shaver J.M (2009) Confounding Changes in Averages with Marginal Effects: Anchoring within Strategic Investment Assessments.

Shepherd C. and Ahmed P.K (2000) From product innovation to solutions innovation: a new paradigm for competitive advantage European Journal of Innovation Management, Volume 3 . Number 2 . 2000 . pp. 100-106

Shephard R.W and Fare R (1974) The Law of Diminishing Returns. Zeitschrift f/it National6konomie 34, 69--90

Sher and Lee (2004) Information technology as a facilitator for enhancing dynamic capabilities through knowledge management. Information & Management 41 pp 933–945

Shipton, H. (2006) 'Cohesion or confusion? Towards a typology for organizational learning research.' International Journal of Management Reviews, 8 (4), pp. 233-252, EBSCO host Business Source Premier

Singlis T.M and Brown W.J (1995) Culture, Self, and Collectivist Communication Linking Culture to Individual Behavior. Human Communication Research, Vol. 21 No. 3,pp 354-38

Simon, H. von der Gathen, A.and Daus P.W (n.d) Retail Pricing – Higher Profits Through Improved Pricing Processes

Skerlavaj M. Stemberger M. I. Skirinjar. R. And Dimovski. D (2007) Organizational learning culture—the missing link between business process change and organizational performance. Int. J. Production Economics 106 pp 346–367

Slack, N., Chambers, S. & Johnston, R. (2010) Operations management. 6th ed. Harlow: Prentice Hall/Financial Times.

Sørensen H. E (2008) " Why competitors matter for market orientation" European Journal of Marketing Vol. 43 No. 5/6, pp. 735-761

Stier H. & Lewin-Epstein N.(2003) Time to Work:: A Comparative Analysis of Preferences for Working Hours WORK AND OCCUPATIONS, Vol. 30 No. 3, pp302-326

Symons, J. & Stenzel, C. (2007) 'Virtually borderless: an examination of culture in virtual teaming', Journal of General Management, 32 (3), pp.1-17, Business Source Premier

Taylor J.B (2008) The Financial Crisis and the Policy Responses: An Empirical Analysis of What Went Wrong. Professor of Economics, Stanford University and Senior Fellow, Hoover Institution.

Taylor, S. (2007) 'Creating social capital in MNCs: the international human resource management challenge', Human Resource Management Journal, 17 (4), pp. 336–354, Wiley InterScience

Teo T.S.H &Liu J. (2007) Consumer trust in e-commerce in the United States,Singapore and China. Omega 35 The International Journal of Management Science pp 22 – 38.

Tkaczynski A . Rundle-Thiele S.R & Beaumont N. (2009), Segmentation: A tourism stakeholder view. Tourism Management 30 pp169–175

Tobin J. & Rose-Ackerman S (2003) Foreign Direct Investment and the Business Environment in Developing Countries: the Impact of Bilateral Investment Treaties William Davidson Institute Working Paper Number 587

Tom Karp and Thomas I. Tveteraas Helgø (2007) Reality revisited: leading people in chaotic change, Journal of Management Development Vol. 28 No. 2, pp. 81-93

Wang H. (2006) From "user" to "customer": TQM in academic libraries? Library Management Vol. 27 No. 9, pp. 606-620

Wilson H. Daniel E. & Davies I. A (2008) The diffusion of e-commerce in UK SMEs JOURNAL OF MARKETING MANAGEMENT, Vol. 24, No. 5-6, pp. 489-516

Wright D.T. & Burns. N.D. New organisation structures for global business: an empirical study. International Journal of Operations & Production Management,Vol. 18 No. 9/10, 1998, pp. 896-923,

Wuyts, S. Stremersch, S. van den Bulte, S. and Franses P.H. (2004) Vertical Marketing Systems for Complex Products: A Triadic Perspective. Journal of Marketing Research Vol. XLI , pp 479-487

Vaivio J. (1999) Exploring a ' non-financial' management accounting change. Management Accounting Research,10, pp409-437

Van Vuuren K (2001) Beyond the Studio: A Case Study of Community Radio and Social Capital. Australian Community Broadcasting Series ISSN 1445-971X Vol. 1, No. 4

Volery T. and Lord D. (2000) Critical success factors in online education. International Journal of Educational Management Volume: 14 Number: 5 pp: 216-223

Zahra, S.A. (2005) 'A theory of international new ventures: A decade of

research', Journal of International Business Studies, 36 (1), January, pp. 20–28.

Zakaria et al (2004) Working Together Apart? Building a Knowledge-Sharing Culture for Global Virtual Teams. CREATIVITY AND INNOVATION MANAGEMENT. Volume 13Number 1

Zellmer-Bruhn, M. & Gibson, C. (2006) 'Multinational organization context: implications for team learning and performance', Academy of Management Journal, 49 (3), pp. 501-518, EBSCOhost Business Source Premier

ABOUT THE AUTHOR

Kevin Griffiths has over 30 years experience in developing new and emerging organisations in both the commercial and the 'not for profit' sector. He lives in Ireland and travels extensively. He has also published **Management of Eco-tourism and its Perception: A Case Study of Belize**

Contact: kevin@jaffamedia.com

www.ingramcontent.com/pod-product-compliance
Lightning Source LLC
Chambersburg PA
CBHW081451170526
45166CB00008B/2394